SELF ESTEEM WORKBOOK FOR WOMEN

Confidence, Self-love, Inner Strength, and Self-care. Get Rid of Negative Thoughts, Overcome Insecurity, Shyness, and Get an Iron Self-Esteem!

Hypnosis Revolution

© Copyright 2020

All rights reserved

This book is targeted towards offering important details about the subject covered. The publication is being provided with the thought that the publisher is not mandated to render an accounting or other qualified services. If recommendations are needed, professional or legal, a practiced person in the profession ought to be engaged.

In no way is it legal to recreate, duplicate, or transfer any part of this document in either electronic means or printed format. Copying of this publication is strictly prohibited or storage of this document is not allowed. Unless with written authorization from the publisher. All rights reserved.

The details supplied herein is specified, to be honest, and constant. Because any liability, in regards to inattention or otherwise, by any usage or abuse of any directions, processes, or policies confined within is the sole and utter obligation of the recipient reader. Under no circumstances will any form of legal duty or blame be held against the publisher for any reparation, damages, or financial loss due to the information herein, either directly or indirectly. The author owns all copyrights not held by the publisher.

The information herein is provided for educational purposes exclusively and is universal. The presentation of the data is without contractual agreement or any kind of warranty assurance.

All trademarks inside this book are for clarifying purposes only and are possessed by the owners themselves, not allied with this document.

Disclaimer

All erudition supplied in this book is specified for educational and academic purposes only. The author is not in any way in charge of any outcomes that emerge from utilizing this book. Constructive efforts have been made to render information that is both precise and effective, however the author is not to be held answerable for the accuracy or use/misuse of this information.

Foreword

I will like to thank you for taking the very first step of trusting me and deciding to purchase/read this life-transforming book. Thanks for investing your time and resources on this product.

I can assure you of precise outcomes if you will diligently follow the specific blueprint I lay bare in the information handbook you are currently checking out. It has transformed lives, and I strongly believe it will equally transform your own life too.

All the information I provided in this Do It Yourself piece is easy to absorb and practice.

Table of Contents

INTRODUCTION 10
CHAPTER ONE 12
  Understanding Self Esteem..12
    The Building Blocks of Self-Esteem...13
    Establish Your Self Esteem 18
    How Can Women's Self Defense Help Your Self Esteem.........26
CHAPTER TWO 29
  Why Self-Esteem 29
    Self-Esteem: Why Do Most Women Find It Difficult to Believe in Themselves? 30
    Signs of Women with Low Self-Esteem...................................32
    Reason for Violence, Anger and Low Self Esteem 37
CHAPTER THREE 47
  Knowing Yourself (Self-awareness) 47
    The Inherent Value Of Knowing Your Strengths 48
    Love Yourself Unconditionally 50
    Understanding Your Core Beliefs...56
CHAPTER FOUR 67
  Defusing Painful Thought 67
    Watching Your Thoughts 69
    Distancing from the Critic 76
    Structure Self-Esteem By Changing Negative Thoughts 80
    Clear Away Negative Thoughts..85

Women Gaining Self Confidence Through Self-Improvement And Positive Thought 102

Cognitive Defusion Intervention 107

Moderating impacts of self-esteem. 114

CHAPTER FIVE 117

Self Esteem and Confidence 117

How You Can Gain Self Confidence. 121

Your Brain on Confidence. 127

Common Barriers to Confidence 128

Ways For Women to Improve Confidence 133

CHAPTER SIX 139

Identify your Stressor 139

The Common Causes of Anxiety and Depression In Women Today. 142

Why Women Suffer From Depression 146

Your Body and Mind Need Stress Relief 153

CHAPTER SEVEN 164

Goal Setting and Planning. 164

Conquering Low Self Esteem 166

Actions For Boosting Low Self-Esteem 175

CHAPTER EIGHT 185

Self-Hypnosis, Meditation, and Affirmation for Women 185

Standing Up For Yourself - What Are Your Limitations? 188

Ten Powerful Ways to Stand Up for Yourself in Any Situation 195

How to Change Negative Thinking and Create a Positive Life 202

Do Self Esteem Affirmations Work? 212

Affirming Your Worth 214

CHAPTER NINE 221

Visualization 221

Mindfulness Meditation 233

Heartfulness Attitudes 236

CHAPTER TEN 248

Acknowledge and Accept Positive Qualities 248

CHAPTER ELEVEN 254

Responding to Criticism 254

CONCLUSION 283

INTRODUCTION

Why build self-esteem? The benefits of having self-confidence are many. Self-esteem is highly related to happiness, psychological strength, and motivation.

Those lacking self-esteem tend to experience anxiety more, problems, anger, persistent pain, and a variety of other distressing physical and emotional symptoms. Morris Rosenberg, Ph.D., the primary researcher on self-confidence, said it well when he mentioned that nothing could be more stressful than the experience of not having the standard anchor and guarantee of a wholesome sense of self-esteem.

This book is written to give readers a more straightforward and quicker way to increasing self-esteem-- one that I hope you will find it richly rewarding.

Thanks again for choosing this book, make sure to leave a short review on Amazon if you enjoy it, I'd love to hear your thoughts.

CHAPTER ONE

Understanding Self Esteem

Many misconceptions and misunderstandings surround self-confidence.

Let's start by plainly understanding where we are heading in this book. Self-esteem is a realistic and appreciative opinion of oneself and being honestly knowledgeable about our strengths, weak points, and everything in between. Think about a good friend who knows you well and values you, knowing that there is a lot more to you than your shortcoming or faults, and you'll get a sense of what 'appreciative' means.

Genuine self-esteem is the conviction that one is as useful as anyone else, but not more so. On the one hand, we feel a quiet gladness to be who we are and a sense of dignity that comes from understanding that we share what all people possess-- intrinsic worth. On the other hand, those with self- esteem are pure, realizing that everyone has much to learn and that we are all in the same boat. It's not necessary to be arrogant or boastful; no need to think that we are more rewarding as a person than others or more important or competent than we are.

Self-confidence is not the same as being self-centered, self-soaked up, or selfish. Can a criminal have high self-esteem? It is essential to distinguish the external appearance of self-esteem from the peaceful, constant, inner gladness that identifies self-esteem.

Self-esteem is not complacency or overconfidence, both of which can set us up for failure. Self-esteem is a very strong motivator to work hard. And self-respect is not only crucial for people in Western cultures; research studies have revealed that self-esteem is connected to the mental health and happiness of adults in diverse cultures, consisting of Asian and Middle Eastern societies.

The Building Blocks of Self-Esteem.

Self-esteem rests on three essential factors or foundation. The first two blocks, worth and unconditional love make up the foundation for the third block; growth. Usually, growth proceeds more effectively as much as the first two blocks are firmly in place.

Building Block 1: Unconditional Worth.

A standard premise is that all people have equal, immeasurable, unvarying intrinsic worth as a person. Worth in an individual is neither made nor increased or decreased by external elements, such as the way you are treated by people, bad decisions, or fluctuations in your bank account balance. Agreed, this is not the message one hears in the market or in some social circles, which designate worth based on monetary or social status. Still, the presumption of equal value as a person is not a new one, and it can be rather empowering. Even intense people might deal with this idea, given that they have been given the message that inner worth can increase or fall with performance or circumstances. So I've found that the following example helps. Perhaps you can picture a round crystal, having facets that refract light beautifully.

The said crystal represents the core worth of each person. The facets consist of the capacities to like, reason, sacrifice, stand firm, beautify and experience beauty, and make the right decisions.

The core self might also be compared to a seed. Think of a newborn. Like that seed, the infant is currently entire, possessing in embryo every attribute needed to thrive. The infant is total, yet not finished (that is, not perfect or thoroughly developed).

Externals.

Externals are outer occasions or situations that can change the way we experience our worth but do not alter our worth. Certain externals or experiences can camouflage or conceal one's core worth, like a dark cloud or haze that surrounds and obscures it. Maybe one has been emotionally, physically, or sexually mistreated. Such treatment by other people can lead one to believe that a person is faulty at the core, even though the focus is worthwhile and whole. Likewise, people who have experienced injuries such as rape or fight often feel shattered inside. Still, they can take advantage of the help of specially trained injury counselors to again feel whole or healed.

Other externals imitate sunshine, brightening our core worth and helping us to experience that worth with complete satisfaction. Being cherished by others or effectively finishing an essential task helps us experience our worth more extremely, which feels good.

Externals-- whether bad or good-- are not the core. If a person equates his/her core human worth to the value of his/her financial investment portfolio (example of external), then that person's self-esteem will fluctuate with the stock exchange, ranging like a roller rollercoaster. Our goal in this chapter is to separate the core value from the externals. Imagine that the cloud around the crystal (core worth) is separated from the glass and moved far from it, representing the reality that core worth is independent of externals.

Externals consist of the state of one's body (health, look, and vigor), financial status, gender, race, age, job title, promos, awards, relationship, family or adversity (marriage or dating status, variety of children, working level of household), appeal, school grades, errors, moods, task or athletic performance, ability levels, and control over events. It can be challenging to separate core worth from externals when the media suggests that one is less than rewarding if one isn't useful, productive, young, and lovely. "The culture we presently have does not make people feel great about themselves. And you have to be strong enough to say if the culture doesn't work, don't buy it." Then we are alleviated of the need to compete to establish worth when we are sure of our equivalent intrinsic worth. We are less likely to be judgemental of ourselves and compare ourselves to others. In short, we become more safe and secure in our worth, and therefore in ourselves.

In some cases, extremely bright people have difficulty separating inner worth from externals. They ask how somebody can have worth when others do not value them or when they feel so useless. We adults can also decide to value our inherent worth and capabilities.

Establish Your Self Esteem

Self-esteem is a mixture of self-worth, self-integrity, self-regard, and self-esteem. It is a mental concept used to explain how somebody feels about his/herself. High self-esteem means a high worth placed on oneself, while low self-esteem implies the opposite.

Abraham Maslow thinks that psychological health and wellness is based on the core, as well as it is just possible whenever the important emphasis of the person is approved, delighted in, and also valued by others and by him or herself. Jack Canfield ones stated: "Self-esteem is based on the feeling of being capable and lovable."

Self-confidence and self-image are related. The term self-image is made use of to clarify a person's mental image of himself-- self-image causes self-worth.

During very early childhood, we establish mental images of ourselves: that we are, what we are proficient at, exactly how we look, and what our strengths and also weaknesses can be. Our experiences and also our interactions with various other people will certainly make these mental pictures stronger inside us. In time these mental self-images will create our concept of self-esteem. Self-esteem involves the sensation that we generate inside ourselves as an outcome of exterior elements. Self-esteem pertains to how much we feel accepted, liked, and also valued by others as well as simply exactly how much we take, like, as well as worth ourselves. It is the mix of those two aspects that shape our self-confidence.

Self-esteem is commonly defined in terms of how we assess ourselves as well as our characteristics. Excellent self-worth implies that we have sufficient confidence not to need the authorization of others.

How is it Developed?

Self-worth starts to develop as early as a youth, and also elements that affect it include the similarity one's understandings and also thoughts, just how other individuals respond, experiences at the institution, job and also the area, impairment, illness, injury, society, religious beliefs, as well as one's function and also the condition in culture.

When the individual doesn't see himself as having the high qualities he admires, low self-confidence is created. Because they set their self-image that means, persons with reduced self-worth normally do have the high qualities they appreciate, but they can't see it.

How Important is Self Esteem?

According to Brian Tracy: "Your self-esteem is possibly the most important component of your personality. Your level of self-confidence is your level of mental fitness.

Self-esteem is essential for people as it provides more confidence to face life. Self-confidence will enable the person to have more optimism and have more momentum to reach their objectives. People with low self-esteem generally feel inferior and might not perform well under different scenarios. They developed false thoughts that nobody will accept them or like them. On the other hand, individuals with healthy self-esteem can feel excellent about their environment and after that about themselves. They can do things more effectively, and by doing so, they can feel pleased with their accomplishments and about themselves.

Feeling good about ourselves will enable us to enjoy life more. The feeling that we are accepted, liked, and loved, implies we have healthy self-esteem, and this feeling will be reflected in our relationships.

One of the significant causes of damaged relationships is low self-esteem.

Developing self-esteem allows us to welcome joy in our lives. It is this feeling that makes you think that you deserve happiness. It is exceptionally essential to comprehend this belief, the belief that you genuinely are worthy of being happy and fulfilled, because with this belief you can treat people with respect, and goodwill, hence preferring abundant interpersonal relationships and avoiding damaging ones. Having little self-regard can lead people to end up being depressed, to fall short of their potential, or to tolerate violent circumstances and relationships. Numerous studies reveal that low self-esteem causes Stress, depression, and anxiety. Research study suggests a positive relationship between healthy self-esteem and many positive results, consisting of joy, humbleness, optimism, and strength. Self-esteem contributes to practically everything you do.

World Health Organization suggests in "Preventing Suicide" released in 2000, that strengthening students' self-esteem is crucial to safeguard children and adolescents against mental distress and sadness, enabling them to cope adequately with challenging and stressful life scenarios. According to Madelyn Swift, our psychological health depends on our self-esteem.

Healthy self-esteem helps you accept yourself and value life, as it is expected to be.

Can You Develop a Healthy Self Esteem?

The reality is, self-esteem is hardly steady. A detailed research study published by the American Psychological Association reported that self-esteem is most affordable among young grownups; however, it increases during adulthood and peaks at age 60, before starting to decline again. On average, women had lower self-esteem than guys did in most of their adult years, but self-esteem levels assembled as men and women reached their 80s and 90s.

The most significant source of self-esteem is your ideas, and these thoughts are within your control. Concentrating on your weak points and errors will establish low self-esteem. You will be able to reverse this type of thinking by focusing instead on your positive aspects and characteristics.

Being a woman is incredible and empowering, although we tend not to have self-esteem. Building self-esteem for women doesn't need to be tough; it will be enjoyable and empowering.

Structure self-confidence for women can be attained in three necessary steps. We tend to must outline who we tend to be.

Secondly, we have a propensity to should choose what we want to attain, and lastly, we tend to produce an arrangement that will sum up our self-esteem and facilitate us to attain our goals.

Building Self Esteem For Girls (Step 1) - Definition

Self-esteem is a word thrown around a lot, but it means different things. To somebody, high self-esteem might mean becoming abundant, whereas to lots of other women, it may mean having the conceit to travel for that task you have always wanted.

The best approach to define what self-esteem means to you is to think of effective women who embody high self-esteem. Thinking of this can help suggest something to you.

When you've got a person in mind, record all of the positive qualities that this particular person embodies. Characteristics like self-esteem and determination are common responses here.

We have a propensity to now have an idea of who we want to be; this is the personification of high self-esteem to us.

We tend to look at what we tend to accomplish.

Building Self Esteem For Women (Step 2) - Dreams With Deadlines

Is there anything you've ever wished to achieve but felt you could not?

Is there something you were told you could not do but wished to?

If you've answered yes to the above questions, you are like lots of women.. Write down everything and anything you want to achieve in your life. Keep in mind; there aren't any boundaries. The only limitations we tend to have are those we tend to enforce upon ourselves!

If you wish to become CEO for a big company, write it down. If you desire to run a marathon, put it down in writing. Whether you believe that you'll be able to or can't do any of these things is unimportant because we tend will tackle that problem next.

Remember to position a due date on your dream. This makes it particular, and your brain likes specifics!

Building Self Esteem For Women (Step 3)- Set Out To Succeed

Now we have a propensity to comprehend who we tend to need to be and what we need to know, we must strive to be successful. We are talking about positive affirmations that make high self-esteem. Building self-esteem for women enables us to beat any barriers and achieve something we wish in our lives.

How Can Women's Self Defense Help Your Self Esteem

Women's self-defense can bring out the lion of a personality that you have deep inside of you. Women's self-defense training can give you the courage to beat the fears that have haunted you for a long time. Your self-esteem will improve, and you will be a much more confident and qualified woman after taking this type of training.

Your self-esteem is necessary. If you do not feel great about yourself, you will not feel great about what you do and how you do it. Women's self-defense helps you to bring in that self-esteem or bring it back into your life. The absence of self-esteem and the fear of new things because of your stress and anxiety due to security can lead you to live a secure life that can prevent you from living life to the fullest.

The self-esteem of that woman is extremely low because she feels that she has to live up to the expectations of that overbearing hubby or boyfriend. A woman's self-defense course will provide an instructor to stand up for herself or defend herself if she is being abused. The self-esteem will increase so much that many women lastly discover the gumption to leave the relationship until counseling and removal is made or to leave the relationship entirely.

You are missing the best part of life if you are scared of being attacked or criticized and go out of your way to avoid possibly unsafe scenarios. Women have prevented going on a trip to a unique location because they hesitate in hazardous situations and their security. They are missing out on a terrific experience because their self-confidence is low, and they do not have the confidence to go and take the leap on that getaway. These women are entrusted with a life filled with disappointing and missed chances. Women's self-defense will give that woman the self-confidence to believe and trust in herself, and by that process, she will take life by the horns.

Such a woman will have more adventures and live life to the fullest. Self-confidence equates to the experience that you will live when you have high self-esteem.

CHAPTER TWO

Why Self-Esteem

When a person has low self-esteem, that means they have negative thoughts on themselves. As we continue this with this book, we are going to discuss why self-esteem is crucial.

Of all, your esteem level all depends on several different factors. How do you see your self-image? You see, there are numerous concerns to ask yourself to determine if you have low self-esteem levels.

Those esteem levels are significant. Why? You are going to think all the time negatively and feel depressed since when they are low. For example, do you think highly of your task? Are you sincerely happy with how your life is?

Why is self-esteem essential?

This is a vital question that has been asked by many people. We are going to tell you what high esteem is, and maybe then, you will know why it is so crucial. When you have a high level, you are going to be very positive in yourself. You are also going to have highly motivated, happy, and have the ideal mindset it requires to succeed.

Self-Esteem: Why Do Most Women Find It Difficult to Believe in Themselves?

From the time you were conceived and brought up in this world, your father and mother or guardian play a vital role in developing your self-esteem. It is because they are the people who make you feel loved and accepted, no matter what or who you are.

Women and Their Lack of Self-Esteem

Have you ever questioned why between a woman and a man, the latter has been continuously the second class resident recently? Today, women around the globe are fighting for equality - equal pay, equal advantages, the same treatment, and similar responsibilities both at work and in the house. There are still many women suffering from low self-esteem, which was caused by beliefs carried over by the generations before them.

Society has taught that as a woman, she must; serve her spouse, take care of the kids, care for her senior parents, make sure the house is spic and span, share in the responsibility of bringing the dough to assist with the daily expenses, to keep everything in order - consultation with the dental professional, kids' activities and practices, costs to pay, errands to do - yet, still manage to keep a smile on her face while handling all these. You feel tired, and all you just want is to get through this life.

" Am I not supposed to be doing these? If I do not do this, who will?"

This is a reasonable question you should have been asking yourself. So you walk around every day of your life managing everything, and instead of feeling good - you feel worn out. You feel old and spent. You feel awful and unwanted. You resigned to your fate that this is how life should be. You are feeling distressed, and you question if you truly deserve something much better in life. This is one sign having low self-esteem.

Signs of Women with Low Self-Esteem

Because worrying is a significant part of what you do, you fret about many things in life. You worry a lot about what others may think about you if you do not do this. You find yourself feeling depressed because of too much worry,

-Nervousness.

There is a worry of saying, acting, and doing in a manner that will trigger embarrassment to yourself and others. You would rather keep to yourself and avoid interactions with other people just to eliminate the possibility of making an error because of this. Of course, no one likes making errors; however - people do make women and errors mainly would beat her self up psychologically and emotionally for longer than necessary because of these errors. There is always a fear that hovers over her head that causes her to feel distressed.

Too many expectations and the desire to be "ideal" cause many women out there to be distressed and disappointed in themselves and others, all this time, we were made to believe that a gorgeous lady is the one who has perfect skin, captivating eyes, an ideal set of teeth, long silky hair, and having a sexy and healthy body. We do everything to be the "perfect" woman, and if we do not reach that expectation despite how unreasonable it is, we scold ourselves.

-Hypersensitivity.

Being too delicate with what others do or state. Any action from others, whether knowingly and unknowingly, would affect you in the wrong method - causing you to feel bad.

-Unhealthy relationships.

Women who discover themselves in and out of bad relationships feel they are not capable and do not deserve a healthy relationship. Women with low self-esteem work harder to keep a male. Due to the feeling of inadequacy, they will compensate and invest more in the relationship. They will go "an additional mile" so their partner won't look elsewhere. There is always the existence of doubts, self-sabotage, and continuous nagging and desiring to be guaranteed all the time since they feel they are not enough. In the end, their partners feel suffocated and desire out.

-Feeling of inadequacy

"I am not good enough," "I can't," I don't understand how" are just a few of the words showing inadequacy and disbelief over your self. Even with other people increasing you up, you stop yourself from accomplishing good things because you "feel" and think that you are not capable.

-Continuous negative self talk.

"I'm always a failure." "I never do the best thing." "I'm silly." "I'm dumb" "I am awful" "I am fat." These negative words are always repeated that even our subconscious mind believes them to be real.

According to psychologists and other specialists, women (and males too) who suffer low self-esteem stem from their youth. How parents see themselves and the environment affect their kids' self-worth. Being ignored, isolated, reprimanded too harshly for any misdeeds, and constant abuse verbally, physically, and mentally are reasons for low self-esteem.

It's time to examine yourself.

Do you suffer from low self-esteem?

Where and to whom does your worth as an individual connected to?

Is it related to achievement, appeal, or your relationships?

If your self worth is reliant on your accomplishment, then you will continuously find yourself doing more and more - accomplishing more and more so that you will feel valued. Time will come; you will see yourself facing the ugly reality that external charm does not last permanently if our self-esteem is based on appeal. You will be annoyed that no matter how difficult you try to preserve your attractiveness and youthfulness - it won't last. If your self-esteem is tied to your relationship, then you will continue to work hard to be the best partner and a caring mom to the point that you will need to compromise yourself at the same time. At the end of all these, you still find yourself not pleased. So the more you will work hard and get what you think is your worth.

Ask yourself this concern: What should you do to attain deep fulfillment and happiness in life?

Everything boils down to your self-esteem. Is it so wrong to live a life based on your authentic self? Do you have to go out and "show" to others that you suffice? What if you get the words "should," "must," or "ought" in your life and do things not because you have to? Can you state that you can live a life based on your real self and not by the need set by other people and society?

We typically see women permitting themselves to be mistreated and taken for granted by the people who make up a vital part of her life. All because they have low self-esteem.

Reason for Violence, Anger and Low Self Esteem

No character quality or condition affects one human that does not impact every human. It is merely a matter of degree.

The other declaration needs to be part of every genuine individual wish to enhance oneself.

Either self-caused or caused on others. That is violence, and so many serene people just love this kind of thing.

Be it Hitler or a little kid who abuses ants; there is a feeling of power in causing discomfort and managing another being. That feeling is the same; it is just a matter of degree figured out by the individual's capabilities. One who feels defenseless has an inner push to feel powerful.

Why are human beings so twisted? Humanity has not been different throughout history. Tortures and atrocities have always become part of our types. In the same vein, all the religions preach about being peaceful as those religious followers go to services and then head out and commit the opposite in the name of that peace-loving god. What can make a human act so inconsistent with what they believe they feel? That is one question we will check out.

On various tracks, let us take a look at a familiar mentor of all religious and magical approaches. To be one with God, you should put all your rely on God alone, quit your ego, and have faith that God will provide all you need. Only with complete unrelenting faith in God can the candidate accomplish unity with the Divine.

That indicates giving up the need, wish, as well as every aspect of attempting to manage the celebrations that happen to you. Manage what comes, yet whatever that could be, approve it as the will of God as well as be content with that.

If it is brief, this one condition is all there is to achieve the experience of expertise even. Your education and learning are going last too if you can be this relying on permanently.

Such a straightforward point, simply one little characteristic of authorization that is all it takes, however so difficult to do, no matter of numerous that have gone through the degree of quitting the world ostensibly, the vast bulk has not given up their need to be in control inwardly.

And right here we have the origin of our suffering; our ego will simply hold despite just how much we wish to. The inner dispute brought on by fragmentation and also managed by barriers and recognition to forget our discomfort, let's time pass remaining in a mindful sleep and even coma to make sure that life can go on. Very little brand-new information up till now, as well as now allows relocate in the direction of a reason and also a possible alternative.

What makes an individual desire to eliminate, ruin, combat, love violence, take pleasure in seeing others suffer? If that is the actual be the question, then the answer is that it is obviously in their character, but how did they get that way?

When we are very young, the response is found in that our personality is formed. We do rarely have a significant change in our character later in life unless a considerable shock prompts us to see what we have is wrong and change. That can happen at any phase in our life depending on your willpower that you are born with; however, it may take a very long time to feel entirely beaten and powerless ultimately. As long as it considers you to give up your need to control, it is as long as you will suffer.

The solution is straightforward, put others before yourself. Pleasant, the kind of response that makes you want to slap the author and demand something helpful! It is hoped that this book will give you enough to work with so that you can effectively understand why that simple instruction is practical and offers more to you than anybody else.

All things are an outcome of several elements or conditions. A kid's innate love integrated with their youthful helplessness to help the one they love produces anger and possibly violence. Also, depending on the character of the child, that could cause an absence of self-esteem because feeling powerless and, for that reason, useless.

The vulnerability can likewise make the adult compensate by demanding so much that they will damage or harm themselves just to be defiant to get their way. The unconscious need to be in control by opposing whatever is presented, good or bad, gives the self-destructive nature. This comes from feeling helpless and not understanding that on the conscious state or level.

Fragmentation sets in when you are feeling unprotected by altering pieces to something else to make sure that you do not see what you are doing or why. Blinded with being rivals and justifying your actions with barriers, you destroy your objectives remarkably promptly. Self-lying now plays its part by verifying through creative thinking that the various other person is a control fanatic or trying to cheat you, or any type of factor to validate your needs, and also buffers than are available in to sidetrack you so that you do not see exactly how you are shedding when you believe you are winning. Regulating another person is not winning; winning is found out by the outcome.

The ego has a considerable component to play in this dealing with barriers and also false coaches who raise the factors for having legal rights, borders, and the demand to be acknowledged as equal and valued.

All this might seem sensible, but only a little objective reasoning is needed to see how this will cause problems and is a demand for other individuals to serve as you want them to fit into your borders. Oddly enough, people seldom turn the tables on their demands and consider how they would feel if being asked the very same points.

The reactions as a result of all this misplaced recognition will lead to disputes, as well as remarkable complications as the various other people can not recognize why one would deliberately cause themselves injuries just to be hard or rigid. This results in a long chain of events in life that take place in our globe with bountiful conflict, Stress, and also temper.

A research study with prisoners has examined and established this to be among the reasons for physical violence.

There are some situations when they have felt so vulnerable that they have been driven to consume alcohol or medications to nonemotional that pain, as well as normally, in an inebriated state, self-constraint is no longer present, and also the fists flew.

Similar scenarios of vulnerability in experiencing injustices have given some individuals a superficial level of self-regard. Just how helpless you are, as well as that is a physical fact, nonetheless, your self worth has just gone down to the bottom due to the fact that you have not acted, you did not even attempt. Perhaps a group of bullies in the institution picked on the nerdy child, and you desired to be a component of the team yet understood that what you are doing is wrong.

What makes somebody intend to eliminate, ruin, fight, love, violence, or love seeing others experience? If that is the concern, the answer is that it is clearly in their character, but exactly how did they get that?

That can occur at any type of stage in our life, depending upon your personal will certainly power that you are birthed with, yet it may take a long period to be defeated and also vulnerable ultimately. As long as it considers you to quit your requirement to control, that will be as long as you will certainly experience.

All things are an outcome of several components or conditions. A child's intrinsic love, integrated with their more youthful vulnerability to aid the one they like produces temper and also possibly physical violence. Or, depending upon the character of the youngster, that might create an absence of self-confidence due to the sensation of vulnerability.

The vulnerability can likewise make the grown-up compensate by requiring a great deal that they will damage or damage themselves simply to be rebellious to get their method. The unconscious requirement to be in control by opposing every little thing, negative or great, provides the suicidal nature. This stems from feeling defenseless and also not comprehending that on the conscious degree.

Fragmentation figures in when you are feeling powerless by switching fragments to something else to ensure that you don't see what you are doing or why. Blinded with being opposite as well as justifying your activities with barriers, you wind up ruining your goals very quickly. Self-doubt currently plays its function by justifying with creativity that the various other individual is a control fanatic or trying to cheat you, or any type of reasons to explain your requirements, and buffers after that are available in to cause some interruption to ensure that you do not see how you are shedding when you believe you are winning.

The vanity has a substantial role to play in this working with barriers and also incorrect mentors, which boost the justifications of having legal rights, borders, as well as the demand to be called equal as well as valued.

All this could appear practical, however, only a little unbiased thinking is required to see exactly how this will trigger disagreement and also is a need for other individuals to act as you desire them to fit right into your borders. Strangely sufficient, individuals seldom transform the tables on their requests as well as consider just how they would certainly feel if being asked the same things.

CHAPTER THREE

Knowing Yourself (Self-awareness)

As you work to grow in different places in your life, it is essential to know yourself truthfully. This is not to say that everything about us needs to change, but it is healthy and perfectly natural to grow in many places.

Knowing yourself can help you in improving your work principles since you can truly know your constraints and know when you are pressing yourself too hard. You've probably had to make yourself step away from your work more than one party. The appeal of achieving objectives and get personal advancement is discovering the balance of work and play.

While it is essential to comprehend your constraints, understanding yourself assists you to know what you can't attain and what you can accomplish. If you've not made a trial, you'll not know how much you can truly achieve.

It is much simpler to keep yourself motivated when you know yourself. When you come in contact with somebody for the first time, and they asked you to motivate them without giving you any details about their lives, you would have a hard time helping them.

How often do you need time to relax? Not just that, you need to understand yourself to have a strong foundation for personal development, but you have to be willing to inspire yourself when things are not right.

The Inherent Value Of Knowing Your Strengths

Strengths, whatever yours are, are action words. Your strengths are evident in your actions.

Strengths are things you develop. deal with, and perfect. When you use or show them, they make you feel capable and not reliable, however natural and at ease.

Knowing about your strengths are using them according to their best advantage is empowering and satisfying. When you're on your side, you should feel essentially gratified, pleasing your inner sanctum, giving joy to your spiritual side while meeting the needs of those around you.

Your strengths in significant areas are up to you. You are the reason your strengths suffer or grow. Knowing your strengths has to do with understanding yourself, not about promoting yourself.

Successful people develop others because they establish themselves first. They find how to handle their weaknesses, and they take risks to build their strengths.

Understanding your strengths doesn't mean you are failing. Knowing your strengths allows you to walk in your calling. It allows you to lead at a high level.

Some people hesitate for their strengths. Some are scared of walking in their talents. By not doing so, they remove the possibility of failure. Along with that, they also turn down the opportunity of success.

Leading from your strengths allows you to invest entirely in yourself, which will enable you to invest adequately in others. Understanding your limitations enables you to do this efficiently.

Love Yourself Unconditionally

The prominent psychologist Abraham Maslow (Lowry 1973) once noted that psychological health and wellness are not feasible without love for the necessary core. Children with self-esteem often tend to have moms and dads who enjoy them.

What is love?
If the core looks like a seed after that love is the nutrition that assists the seed to expand. Also though we may not constantly have the love of others, we can constantly choose to enjoy ourselves.
" Each person has been developed to be as well as like loved"-- Mother Teresa

Foundation 3: Growth
We tend to feel better regarding ourselves when we are living, making reasonable decisions, creating desirable high qualities, and polishing the harsh sides around the core.

We may consider building block 3 as the procedure of putting love right into activity. Expanding does not transform our core well worth, yet it aids us to experience it with higher complete satisfaction. The inner core can expand also as the body ages or ends up being infirm.

Workout: Start with completion in Mind.

Think about a few of the factors that we have checked out so much: Self-esteem is a quiet and also relatively unshakeable sense of satisfaction that stems from acknowledging as well as valuing our existing well worth, and then choosing to love and expand. Instead, one with self-esteem thinks about the wellness of others, along with the health of oneself. Self-confidence can be developed with persistent initiative.

Look after Yourself

Look after Your Mind by Caring for Your Body

Taking good care of the body is a great way to strengthen psychological wellness and also self-confidence because the body and mind are interactively connected.

If we overlook our physical wellness, we can not be our finest emotionally. The silver lining is that (1) we now understand just how to maximize physical health and wellness, and (2) the financial investment of cash, initiative, as well as the time needed to achieve this is very little. Physical health resembles a three-legged stool, which falls if one of the legs is missing out on. The three legs of fitness are workout, rest, as well as nourishment.

Rest

We invest a third of our lives in bed, sleep hasn't been seriously researched up till just recently. Rest deprival has ended up being a whole lot much more common, and we now know that insufficient rest negatively impacts mood, immunity, insulin resistance, levels of anxiety hormonal agents, heart disease rates, power levels, weight gain, memory, traffic accidents, and also job and sports performance.

The majority of adults require even more than 8 hours per night to be and also function at their finest, but the normal grownup gets less than 7 as well as brings a gathered rest financial debt that goes beyond twenty-four hrs. A solitary excellent night's sleep will not repay this sleep financial commitment however will certainly instead tend to make one feel drowsier the following day. You can establish your sleep requires by sleeping as long as you can each evening for several weeks till your rest degrees off at a constant hour.

The 2nd element required for wonderful sleep is consistency.

The brain controls rest rhythms, which weaken as we age. To keep rest cycles normal, we require normal wake-up and retiring times.

Aids to a wonderful night's sleep consist of the following:

- Get a clinical examination to rule out and also diagnose problems that can hinder sleep or trigger daytime exhaustion, including thyroid conditions, diabetes mellitus, anemia, bruxism, hyperventilation, gastroesophageal reflux, or rest problems.

Ask your medical professional for an overnight sleep research study to examine if sleep apnea (or one more sleep disorder) is presumed. Apnea creates daytime sleepiness, anxiousness, and a host of various other illness indications, however, it can be successfully handled.

- Treat depression, stress, and anxiety, or problem anger, all of which can break down sleep—attempt to explain the problem in your diary if you have recurring questions. Then write down a different ending-- anyone you want. Psychologically practice the new dream with its original end for a few minutes daily.

- Create an ideal sleep environment.

Completely darken the room- cover any clock radios that may be discharging light and ensure that the early morning sun does not come through windows. Lessen sounds (use earplugs or white music) and movements (keep animals beyond the bedroom). Maintain a tranquil, soothing sleep environment in your bedroom by using it for just activities that are relaxing. Pay costs, enjoy tv, research study, and talk on the phone in other areas of your house instead of in your bedroom.

- If you seem to derive benefits from naps, take them regularly during the early afternoon if you want to enjoy your naps. This is the time for a siesta in some cultures when the body temperature drops. The advised nap time is from 15 to 120 minutes, with high personal irregularity. Try avoiding naps to consolidate nighttime sleep if taking a nap seems to make it tough for you to sleep at night.

- Try working out before dinner, to allow your body enough time to relax before bed. A workout is the most effective way to reduce the quantity of time needed to fall asleep, to enhance sleep quality and sleep time, and to decrease nighttime awakenings, even in the elderly.

- Reduce or eliminate alcohol, nicotine, and caffeine. These interrupt people's sleep, even when they don't realize it. Attempt to avoid these for a minimum of 4 to 6 hours before retiring.

- Wind down before retiring. Eat dinner early while you keep it light, with a little serving of protein to avoid nighttime appetite. Write down your worries and plan your next day at least an hour before retirement. Turn the lamps to their lowest setting or use available nightlights, to enable your brain to relax (strong lights signal the brain to stay awake). Shut down the phone and tv a minimum of an hour before you go to bed, and after that, retire when you are drowsy, not when the clock says. A warm bath about an hour or more before bedtime promotes sleep.

- Do not rely on sleeping tablets. Instead, use sleep hygiene and skills that lower stress and anxiety, which improve sleep without adverse effects. Effective sleep programs promote sleeping regular hours, rising if you do not fall asleep within half an hour, doing something that is not helping until you are ready to go to bed again, reducing the consumption of liquids at night, practicing relaxation and abdominal breathing, and lowering devastating ideas (such as "It's horrible that I can't drop off to sleep"). As one guru taught, "When exhausted, take sleep." And remember that even an additional twenty minutes of sleep per night can considerably enhance mood and efficiency.

Understanding Your Core Beliefs

The basic structure blocks of self-esteem are your core beliefs: your fundamental assumptions about your worth worldwide.

Core ideas determine to what degree you see on your own as worthy, safe, competent, powerful, autonomous, and also loved. They also establish your feeling of belonging and a basic image of how you are treated by others.

Negative core ideas formulate the rules you utilize daily that claim, "Because I am foolish, I need to not chat in conferences," or "I can never drive a stick-shift since I'm so incompetent." Favorable core ideas verify that you can master algebra since you are qualified and also wise of discovering or that you can ask for a raise since you deserve it.

Your internal monologue is exceptionally affected by your core ideas (" Don't try to fix that plug-- you'll possibly electrocute yourself!"). By the same token, if your self-statements show basic confidence in your knowledge, this core idea will certainly be validated as well as strengthened.

Core beliefs are the real structure of your self-worth: they mainly determine what you can as well as can refrain (expressed as your rules) and how you analyze occasions in your globe (expressed as your stream of consciousness).

Core ideas are frequently misshaped by very early injury as well as deprival. In reaction to injure or rejection, you may have come to see on your own as flawed or not worthy. Because no one mirrored back your worth, now you might simply stop working to see it.

Transforming your core beliefs requires effort and time, as well as yet altering them will essentially modify your sight of on your own as well as your setting. Moving unfavorable core beliefs in extra sensible instructions resembles changing a funhouse mirror with a nondistorting one. Instead of appearing like a three-foot nerd, you see on your own as typically as well as effectively proportioned.

Assist for identifying, testing, and also changing unfavorable core beliefs can be located in our publication Prisoners of Belief (McKay and also Fanning 1991). If you are in a situation, a target of kid abuse, or lack self-motivation, seek the advice of a.

psychological health specialist to assist you in putting these strategies to function.

Determining Core Beliefs.

Familiarizing negative core ideas is the very first step towards altering them. Like the studs and also floor joists of a house, core ideas aren't conveniently apparent, however, everything else rests upon them. If you feel dumb, inexperienced, hideous, like a failing, or negative much of the moment, you might not be promptly mindful of the ideas developing these sensations. However a large amount of what you do, what you think, as well as what you feel will certainly be a straight repercussion of beliefs whose surprise impact touches every quadrant of your life.

To enhance your understanding of your core beliefs, you need to begin maintaining a monologue journal. Such a journal provides you the possibility to tape-record your stream of consciousness-- your self-statements-- at times when you're feeling distressed, mad, depressed, guilty, and more.

This might not be very easy initially. It can be extremely challenging to capture on your own in the act of thinking unfavorable thoughts. Such ideas can be so ingrained that you need to make a specific initiative just to sort them out from the various other "history noise" in your life. Lots of people have a problem, also, separating ideas from feelings. As you'll see in the instance later on in this area, sensations can normally be summed up in 1 or 2 words (" unskilled," "insufficient," "beat"), whereas thoughts are much more challenging, like fragments of overheard dialogue. Taken together, your thoughts comprise your very own stream of consciousness. They serve to enhance and verify your standard core ideas.

Laddering and Motif Evaluation

Whenever you can not keep in mind pieces from your internal monologue, use visualization to recall the specific details of a circumstance (see phase 14). Visualization will boost your memory as well as help provide an accurate account of your feelings as well as self-statements.

After you've videotaped your self-talk for one week, you can assess it to reveal the core ideas that may be sustaining much of it. You can do this by utilizing the strategies of laddering and also motif analysis.

Laddering reveals core ideas via questioning declarations in your monologue journal. The questions offer a method to look methodically for the ideas that underpin your self-statements.

Follow this with an additional concern that examines your response to the first inquiry in terms of its definition for you. The 2nd question should be stated as: "What does that mean to me?"

Currently begin the process of addressing the questions, ending up each round with a repeating of "What does that mean to me?" Like the rungs of a ladder, this procedure of repeating will certainly lead you down into the depths of the core ideas underlying each self-statement. Here's exactly how the process benefited George:

What happens if I am a....? What does that mean to me? It suggests that people will constantly make the most of me.

Suppose individuals will constantly take advantage of me? What does that mean to me? It means that I'll constantly obtain the short end of the stick.

Suppose I constantly obtain the short end of the stick? What does that mean to me? It indicates that I'm a sufferer.

What happens if I am a victim? What does that mean to me? It indicates that I'll never do well in anything I try to do.

George was able to quit below: he'd reached the core idea underlying his overheard thought, "What a chump!".

Avoid addressing your questions in the laddering procedure with sensations (" it implies I'll feel afraid and also overwhelmed"), because it leads no place, as well as does not use your beliefs. Confine your answers instead of statements that reveal presumptions, verdicts, and ideas.

The other strategy for disclosing core beliefs is motif evaluation. This procedure involves browsing for a style that repeats itself throughout most of your problematic circumstances. George saw inexperience or stupidity as a style in much of the situations that made him feel uncomfortable (broken die ... son hurt ... being chewed out by employer).

Susie, a part-time registered nurse, read over her checklist of bothersome scenarios that triggered anxiety or clinical depression.

Buying a secondhand car.

Phil is not being activated by me. Attempting to ask for a raise.

Trying to take care of issues concerning my daughter's behavior at college. Examining a doctor's orders for the patient's benefit.

When Susie reviewed this listing, she identified a fundamental belief that she is helpless, that she is unable of fixing issues, obtaining her demands satisfied, as well as successfully handling a difficulty.

Her matching self-talk confirmed this core belief of being vulnerable, weak (" simply a lady ... it'll be incorrect ... he'll never pay attention to you ... it's like shouting in the wind").

You can reveal core ideas by analyzing your diary in this way. Browse for themes suffusing bothersome scenarios and also compose them down.

Knowing Your Rules.

Complying with exercises will certainly help you recognize the unspoken rules you've developed to maintain your behavior and feelings in line with your core ideas. Emphasis on the one that seems to have the most adverse impact on your self-esteem if you uncovered more than one core idea in the last workout. Does this belief make you assume you're a failure, unsightly, inexperienced, unworthy? It's time to service transforming this belief.

Sadly, a core belief is so subjective that you can not examine it directly. You can evaluate the rules derived from them. Streaming from each core idea is a plan for just how to live your life, just how to prevent pain and catastrophe. For instance, if you believe that you're a failure, your policies may consist of the following: Never try anything hard. Never ask inquiries. Never expect to get ahead. Never experiment with sporting activity groups. Never quit a task. Never test another's point of view. If you believe that you are unworthy, regulations for a living might consist of the following: Never ask for anything. Always work added difficulty. Never claim no to anything. Always make every effort to be perfect. Never admit a mistake or blunder. Never initiate a call with someone you find eye-catching.

CHAPTER FOUR

Defusing Painful Thought

Sometimes the pathological critic seems relentless. Undeterred by your attempts at accurate thinking, the critic piles it on. One attacking thought follows another in the process called chaining. And each of these linked thoughts has a theme—your flaws and failures. After even a few minutes of chaining, the pain starts. Your mood and self-esteem plummet.

These are the times when rebutting the critic doesn't seem enough. The thoughts come at you with speed and believability that overwhelm your resolve to resist them. But there is a way to meet and overcome this challenge. It's called defusion. Developed as a core process in acceptance and commitment therapy, defusion is a strategy to gain distance and perspective in the face of ruminative thoughts. Instead of "fusing" with self-attacking cognitions, you can use defusion to help you observe and then let go of the most upsetting mental chatter.

You will learn to watch your mind as if it were a popcorn machine, spouting thought afterthought. Then you'll learn to label, let go, and distance from self- judgments, taking them less seriously as they parade across your mental screen. Instead of being your thoughts ("I'm stupid," or "I'm boring"), you can learn merely to have a thought ("I'm having a thought that I'm stupid," or "I'm having a thought that I'm boring"). Notice the difference: "I'm stupid" leaves no room for doubt, and fuses your identity with being intellectually inferior. "I'm having the thought that I'm stupid" is merely an idea, not reality. Your core self and the idea of stupidity remain separate.

You have 60,000 thoughts a day. They are products of your mind—not important, not necessarily true. You can learn, through defusion techniques, to just let them pass and drift away. These thoughts are nothing more than well-worn neural pathways, and the techniques you'll learn in this chapter will help you stop buying into all those old putdowns and judgments.

Watching Your Thoughts

Defusion begins with observing your mind. There are two ways to learn this—a simple exercise called the white room meditation can help you watch your mind and see what it does. Mindful focusing can also allow you to observe mental processes.

White Room Meditation

Imagine that you're in an entirely white room—walls, floor, and ceiling. On your left is an open doorway; on your right is another open doorway. Now, assume that your thoughts are coming in from the doorway on your left, passing in front of you, and exiting the room from the doorway at your right. As your thoughts cross the room, you can give them a visual image—birds flying, an animal running—or you can simply say "thought" as they enter. Don't analyze or get attached to any thought. Just allow each to have a brief moment in front of you before it leaves through the right-hand doorway.

Some thoughts seem urgent and demand more attention. They somehow tend to stick around longer than others. Some thoughts are persistent and show up over and over again. This is how thoughts often are, persistent. Simply notice them and let them go. Turn your attention to the next thought and the next. Do the meditation for five minutes, and notice what happens. Do your thoughts slow down or speed up? Do they feel more or less urgent? How hard was it to let go and turn to the next thought? The mere act of observing thoughts often has the effect of slowing them down and making you feel calmer. But however the meditation makes you feel, the important thing is learning to watch your popcorn machine mind.

Mindful Focusing

This technique draws from Buddhist practices that go back for thousands of years. It starts by just noticing the breath, following it in through the nose, down the back of your throat, into the lungs, and down to where your diaphragm stretches and releases. As you make each out-breath, count—1 on the first outbreath, 2 on the second, and so on till you reach 4. On the fourth outbreath, start your count over at 1.

As you focus on your breath, you'll inevitably have thoughts. You can use the experience of watching your breath as an opportunity to also be aware of what your mind is doing. As each thought arises, acknowledge it (there's a thought) and then bring your attention back to your breath. The full sequence for mindful focusing is (1) watch and count your breaths, (2) notice when a thought shows up, (3) acknowledge the thought, and (4) go back to noticing and counting each breath.

Do five to ten minutes of mindful focusing every day for a week. Watching how thoughts show up, while each time returning to the breath, is a good way to observe your mind. No matter how hard you try to stay focused on the breath, your mind will keep "popping" thoughts. You'll also notice how some thoughts seem urgent and harder to let go of.

Labeling Thoughts

Another way to gain distance from your thoughts is to label them. Types of labeling include:

I'm having a thought that... Each time your critic hits you with a negative thought, repeat the thought with that phrase: I'm having a thought that I'm ugly. I'm having a thought that nobody likes me. As noted earlier, labeling thoughts in this way makes them feel less urgent and believable. They are, after all, just thoughts.

Now my mind is having a thought... Specific labels for this exercise might include "fear thoughts," "judgment thoughts," "not-good-enough thoughts," or "mistake thoughts." You can make up your labels, but the important thing is to use the phrase: Now my mind is having a thought because it creates distance between you and the thought. Try the white room meditation again, but this time, label each thought that shows up. Notice how labeling changes the experience of observing your mind.

Thank you, Mind... Thank you, Mind, for that judgment thought. The idea here is to recognize that your mind is trying to help with these thoughts. You can express appreciation (further distancing from the cognition) while labeling the type of thought your mind has given you.

Letting Go of Thoughts

Now that you're better able to notice and label critical thoughts, the next—and most important—step is to let go of them. Most "letting go" strategies involve imagery that somehow creates more and more physical distance from the thought—until it disappears. The following are a few examples, but you can easily make your own.

Leaves on a stream. Imagine critical thoughts to be autumn leaves falling from a tree. They drop into a swiftly moving stream that sweeps around a bend and out of sight.

Balloons

Imagine a clown holding an array of red helium balloons. As each thought arrives, attach it to a balloon that soars up and floats away in the sky.

Trains and boats. See yourself at a railroad crossing as a freight train rolls by. Attach critical thoughts to each car passing in front of you. Conversely, imagine yourself on a riverbank, and conceive each thought as a boat passing in front of you and out of sight.

Billboards

See each thought displayed on a billboard, one after another, on a long stretch of highway. As each new thought appears, the old billboard (and its thought) is left behind.

Computer pop-ups

In the same way, pop-up advertisements suddenly appear on your computer, imagine critical thoughts popping up on a screen. When the next thought arrives, the old pop-up disappears.

Some individuals find it easier to let go by doing something physical:

Turning the hand

Hold your hand out, palm upward. As you notice and label each thought, imagine it sitting in your palm. Now slowly rotate your hand until the palm faces down. Imagine the thought dropping from your hand and disappearing out of sight. Repeat the process for each new thought.

Taking a breath

As the critic strikes, take a deep breath and notice the painful thought. Then, as you exhale, let the thought go and disperse in the air.

Combining Watching, Labeling, and Letting Go

It's time to put these components together. The priority is to be alert to the critic. Noticing the attacking thought, when it comes, is how you stop chaining and start defusing. You can often recognize the critical voice by how it affects your mood. As soon as you start to feel down or deflated, pay attention to your thoughts.

Now label the thought: I'm having the thought that…or I'm having a thought. As previously discussed, this is important because it creates distance from the cognition and reminds you that it's just something in your mind.

Lastly, choose a visualization or physical response (turning your hand, taking a breath) to help you let go. It's often effective to have one of each—a visualization of the thought floating away and a physical experience that promotes the same thing.

Distancing from the Critic

Now that you are beginning to watch, label, and let go of self-attacking thoughts, some advanced defusion skills can further distance you from the critic.

Thought repetition. Research shows that merely repeating a thought out loud reduces its power to hurt you. Take, for example, the self-judgment, "I'm a bad father." Its power derives from forgetting this is a thought and assuming it's the truth. If you repeat "I'm a bad father," fifty times or more, something important happens. The words lose their meaning; they become mere sounds. Try it yourself. Take a recent attack from your critic and condense it into a sentence of a few words. Now repeat those words out loud until they feel emotionally dead, without importance. Notice how they now seem like a sequence of sounds stripped of meaning. Any time you want, you can repeat the critic's words until they lose their punch.

Card-carrying

When a self-attacking thought shows up, you can get emotional distance by writing it down and carrying the card with you. Each time the thought reoccurs, you can remind yourself, "I have that thought, and I don't need to think about it now."

Objectifying thoughts

The goal here is to give a thought physical properties: How big is it? What color? What shape? What does it feel like? How does it sound? Tony tried objectifying him I'm stupid though. He imagined it as a big, gray medicine ball, heavy with a sandpaper texture. It made a thumping sound as it dropped. When Tony turned I'm stupid into a thumping medicine ball, the thought seemed less important.

Silly names and voices

When a critical thought shows up frequently, try giving it a ridiculous name. Tony started referring to thoughts about his intelligence as medicine ball thoughts. Other examples are "stink bomb thoughts," "dark and stormy thoughts," "dear old Dad thoughts," "Raggedy Anne thoughts," and so on. Make the names as silly or as absurd as possible.

You can also use silly or mocking voices to make fun of critical thoughts. Tony used a newscaster voice to mock his attacking thoughts: "Tony's medicine ball voice gave him a beating at work today." Tony, as a child, was entertained by his father's Donald Duck imitations. Now he began using that voice himself to say out loud his critical thoughts.

Another technique is to sing (to familiar tunes like "Home on the Range") some of your self-attacks. "You, you are the worst— nitwit to walk on the earth," Tony sings and then starts laughing.

The three questions. When you suffer the same self-critical thought, over and over, try asking the following three questions:

How old is this thought? Did it start following a breakup? After a job loss? Does it go back to high or middle school? If you aren't sure, just make a rough guess when it started.

What's the function of the thought? Ask yourself this question: What pain is this thought trying to help you avoid? Feeling ashamed or bad about yourself? Feeling afraid of rejection or contempt from others? Feeling wrong or defective? Feeling sad about a mistake or a failure? Every thought has a purpose, and oft-repeated thoughts usually show up in the service of avoiding chronic emotional pain.

How is the thought working? If you've had the thought a long time and its purpose is to help you avoid pain, is the thought of doing its job? Are you less ashamed or afraid of rejection? Do you feel less defective, less like a failure? Or is this pain as big and hard to feel as ever?

Here's another question: Is the thought causing pain rather than protecting you? Does it make you feel worse about yourself— more ashamed, more afraid, sadder? If that's the case, your thought is a "double whammy." It's failing in its purpose and doing damage, besides.

Structure Self-Esteem By Changing Negative Thoughts

You might be giving yourself negative messages about yourself. Lots of people do. These are messages that you found out when you were young. You learned from various sources, including other kids, your instructors, member of the family, caregivers, even from the media, and from prejudice and stigma in our society.

Once you have discovered them, you may have repeated these negative messages over and over to yourself, especially when you were not feeling well or when you were having a tough time. You may have believed them. You might have even worsened the problem by making up some negative messages or ideas of your own. These damaging thoughts or words make you feel bad about yourself and decrease your self-esteem.

Some examples of common negative messages that individuals repeat over and over to themselves include: "I am a jerk," "I am a loser," "I never do anything right," "No one would ever like me," I am a klutz." The majority of people believe these messages, no matter how false or unbelievable they are. They show up instantly in the ideal scenario. For example, if you get a wrong answer, you think, "you are so silly." They might consist of words like should, ought, or must. The messages tend to envision the worst in everything, especially you, and they are tough to shut off or unlearn.

You may think these ideas or give on your own these adverse messages so usually that you are rarely conscious of them. Bring a little pad with you as you go around your day-to-day regimen for some days as well as make a note of negative concepts about on your own whenever you notice them.

It assists to take a more in-depth check out your negative thought patterns to look into whether or not they hold. You might require a buddy or specialist to help you with this. When you are in the ideal frame of mind as well as when you have a favorite way of thinking regarding on your own, ask on your own the following questions about each unfavorable thought you have observed:

- Is this message actual?

- Would a person claim this to another person? Otherwise, why am I stating it to myself?

- What do I maintain believing this belief? If it makes me feel dreadful about myself, why not quit considering it?

You may additionally ask an additional individual, someone who likes you, and also who you rely on if you must believe this concerning yourself. Often, merely having a look at a thought or scenario in new light aids.

The following step in this procedure is to establish favorable declarations you can claim to yourself to transform these adverse thoughts whenever you discover yourself believing them. You can not be feeling a negative one when you are thinking about a positive thought concerning yourself.

Stay clear of using adverse words such as stress, scared, distressed, weary, bored, not, never, can't. Rather, state, "I concentrate on the positive" or whatever seems appropriate to you. Always use today's tense, e.g., "I am healthy, I am well, I am pleased, I have an excellent work," as if the problem already exists.

You can do this by folding a note in half, the excellent way of making 2 columns. In one column, compose your unfavorable idea, as well as in the other column, write a favorable feeling that opposes the adverse idea as shown on the following page.

You can handle transforming your adverse thoughts to positive ones by:

- Replacing the negative idea with the positive one every single time you recognize you are thinking of the negative sensation.

- Repeating your favorable reasoning over as well as over to yourself, out loud whenever you obtain an opportunity as well as also sharing them with one more individual ideally.

- Writing them over as well as over.

- Making indicators that state the positive thought, hanging them in areas where you would certainly see them often-like on your fridge door or the mirror in your bathroom-and duplicating the thought to yourself long times when you see it.

Negative Thought	Positive Thought
I am not worth anything.	I am a valuable person.
I have never accomplished anything.	I have accomplished many things.
I always make mistakes.	I do many things well.
I am a jerk.	I am a great person.
I don't deserve a good life.	I deserve to be happy and healthy.
I am stupid.	I am smart.

It helps in strengthening the positive thought if you repeat it over and over to yourself when you are genuinely relaxed, like when you are doing a deep-breathing or relaxation workout, or when you are just falling asleep or getting up.

Changing the negative ideas you have about yourself to positive ones takes some time and persistence. If you use the following strategies regularly for 4 to 6 weeks, you will discover that you don't think these unfavorable thoughts about yourself. You can repeat these activities if they repeat themselves some other time. Do not quit. You are best to believe great ideas about yourself.

These few recommendations are just the commencement of the journey. As you deal with building your self-esteem, you will observe that you feel better a developing frequently, that you are enjoying your life more than you did in the past, in which you are doing more of the things you have always wanted to do.

Clear Away Negative Thoughts

Self-esteem allows us to experience ourselves precisely and happily. What prevents us from doing so? Unreasonably bad ideas-- which surround and camouflage the core like a cloud of particles after a storm. Cognitive therapy (CT) refers to the branch of psychology that helps people determine, challenge, and then change such thoughts. This well-researched technique is considered a mainstream treatment for depression, issue, and stress and anxiety anger. Because self-esteem is so highly related to these conditions, Cognitive therapy is also beneficial for self-esteem structure.

Albert Ellis, Ph.D., and Aaron Beck, MD (1976), (Ellis and Harper 1975) developed similar techniques for helping people in reshaping their thinking routines. Their techniques illustrate the way thoughts affect our feelings as follows: Adversity, Thoughts, Emotions

Adversity implies a distressing situation or event. For example, assuming that Paula and Lisa grew up with an extremely abusive father. In response to such abuse (hardship), Paula thinks, "I've been dealt with so inadequately. Lisa responds to the same kind of violence with different thoughts. What determines whether we experience some form of anger or disturbance at the emotional level is the ideas that we choose.

Cognitive Therapy shows that the thoughts affecting our emotions travel through our minds so rapidly that we barely see them, let alone stop to check them for reasonableness. Dr. Beck calls these automated ideas (ATs). ATs that are unreasonably negative judgmental, unkind, and inaccurate ideas that make us feel unpleasant and dissatisfied with ourselves-- are called distortions.

Cognitive Therapy suggests that individuals are unbelievably reliable in insensible reasoning. Think about, for instance, what children assume of where infants stem from before they have all the truths. Their reasoning finishes up being extra affordable when they obtain truths.

Cognitive Therapy asserts that individuals can promptly as well as properly uncover to know their idea patterns, test them, and after that change distortions with even more sensible concepts. As they do so, they acquire an action of control over both their concepts as well as their feelings.

Our reasoning patterns, for good or negative, are affected by some reason. For example, the occasions we experience can impact our thoughts. Thus, someone who is overused sexually or physically might think, "I was taken care of as a point, so I require to be one." One's social setting, which may include the media, one's buddies, and also one's household, can likewise influence the way we assume. A daddy might welcome his little girl on finding out that she has been raped as well as just say, "That demand to have been so hard." If he rather evaluated her or questioned her motives, just how various the daughter's ideas would be.

The emotions and also self-confidence of soldiers can be affected by the support they experience upon returning from battle. Our physical condition, our state of wellness, or how rested, nourished, and conditioned we are, additionally impacts our capability to think plainly. Our coping abilities as well as behavior patterns can influence our thinking. Events can change our reasoning, a typical presumption of

Cognitive Therapy is that we are eventually accountable for the ideas that we select. We can't constantly control the method others treat us. We are completely free to manage our ideas. This presumption does not condemn people for doing not have self-esteem. Rather, it equips us to recognize that we can form the suggestions that influence self-esteem as well as stay clear of criticizing others for our existing problems.

= All-or-nothing thinking

Right here you hold on your own as high as feasible, or near-perfect, conventional. If you quit working to "clear the bar," you end that you are worthless. There is no center ground or partial credit report for the initiative.

Others may examine their worth ought to they quit functioning to make a particular wage, lose a disagreement, or make a mistake. You may think, "I batted concerning 8 hundred on this job.

= Labeling.

Have you ever before observed that individuals typically label themselves wrongly? (Notice that this last utterance isn't a worry as much as it is an expression of animosity. You could ask if such unkind judgments serve to encourage as well as motivation does.

In another way, you might think, "A loser never wins, so why attempt?".

Right here's why a negative tag is unreasonable. When you state, "I am dumb (or dumb, or boring)," you are stating that you are dumb always as well as in every scenario. Others might reveal intelligence with individual (emotional knowledge) abilities, social (people) capacities, music, art (or other spatial capacities), or body capacities (such as sporting activities or dance).

Overgeneralizing.

Ask a pessimist or a person with low self-confidence to go over why he got into a debate with his partner, and he is most likely to state something like "I'm not exceptionally quick" (providing himself a tag). He is probably to make it even worse by believing, "I constantly ruin connections. Rodney Dangerfield quipped that his psychiatrist rapidly told him, "Don't be absurd to believe, "Sometimes, I do reasonably well. Some individuals like me, a minimum of rather.".

Yes," you might assume, "but I recognize that the waitress disapproval of me. You will certainly not recognize if he does feel that means unless you find it out. You might think that if you go to the block party everybody will dislike you as well as you'll have an undesirable time.

= Emotional Reasoning.

Currently, when you encounter a brand-new and difficult situation, do you still feel poor and therefore believe that you are insufficient? When you made a foolish decision as well as felt so embarrassed that you wrapped up that you are pointless, or possibly.

Advise yourself that adverse sensations are signals of distressed, not declarations of reality. The difficulty the underlying ideas. Asking "What would 100 percent inadequate, pointless, or poor be like?" helps you to stay clear of all-or-nothing thinking.

= Dwelling on the adverse.

One plant is abstaining from doing so well, so you concentrate solely on that having a difficult time plant. When you find on your residence on what's incorrect in yourself or your life, you may think, "Okay, perhaps this is something I can deal with. Possibly the pleased individual is making an effort to see the larger photo and also worth what isn't incorrect.

= Turning down the Positive.

Whereas residence on the negative overlooks positives, this distortion negates positives. Envision that a person compliments you are doing an outstanding job.

= Making Negative Comparison.

How satisfying it can be to apply ourselves, invest our skills, and also attain objectives connected to pastimes, education, career, recreation, meaningful causes, or connections. The examples established by those we appreciate and also respect can influence us and recommend opportunities. A problem emerges, nonetheless, when we begin to compare ourselves to others. In each case, we get the brief end of the stick, and also self-confidence experiences.

The remedy to this distortion is to simply stop comparing and recognize that everyone contributes in unique ways at his/her exceptional speed. I'll ask my trainees, "Who is more important, a cosmetic surgeon or a basic practitioner?" They may address, "Well, a cosmetic surgeon might fix a severe crisis, but the family doctor might avoid it from taking place." "Who is more beneficial, a surgeon or a physical therapist?" I ask. "Well, the surgeon can conserve life, but the therapist might help to restore physical function and hope," they react. When we consider who is more crucial to the country's health, the doctor, or the garbage collector, we quickly know that people contribute in different ways. Why must we compare and judge? As we step back to see the larger picture, we begin to see that everyone has a diverse mixture of weaknesses and strengths. As we make comparisons of ourselves to shining examples of success, we can keep in mind that each person, even a specialist, struggles in particular places.

Shoulds, Musts, and Oughts

"Should" statements are perfectionistic, rigid needs that we make of ourselves, possibly hoping that such demands will help us to overcome the discomfort of being imperfect. We'd expect that these demands would motivate us to do much better; they usually make us feel worse. Research study recommends that we tend to perform better when we make every effort to do a great job, not a perfect job because we are not as uptight when we are just attempting to do a good job.

What would it suggest if you didn't achieve what you feel that you must or should? Would it suggest that you wear, or just imperfect? Possibly the only sensible "require to" tells us that we have to be as we are, given our insufficient background, experience, capability degrees, and also understanding. Some would certainly say that a kinder, as well as a more effective way to encourage people, is to alter the requirements with "would certainly," "could," "wish," "favor" as well as "pick" affirmations. Rather than stating "I should," "I ought to," or "I must," we might believe "I desire to boost" "I pick to work hard," "I would certainly love to win the competition," "I want to be a caring mom and dad," "It would certainly be wonderful to reach that goal," or "I ask exactly how I could enhance; what would it take?" Please understand, though, that "have to" statements can be challenging to launch. It typically aids to understand that giving up the "must" does not mean quitting a treasured value, such as doing or aiming one's finest. It simply releases us to come close to the objective in a more satisfying, much less judgmental, as well as, we wish, a more efficient way.

= Catastrophizing.

We may assume, for example, "I would never state a word. When we quit catastrophizing, we end up being calmer as well as think more plainly. Catastrophizing is tested by thinking, "Okay, I do not like this, however, I can most certainly bear it," "It maybe even worse.

= Personalizing.

Customizing is thinking that you are a lot more involved or liable than the truths revealed. A rape target usually believes that the crime is her mistake, instead of the failure of the offender. Or a guy may question what he did to deserve his partner's dismayed outbursts, not understanding that his partner surged at the world that day.

Paradoxically, the effort backfires, thinking about that reality encourages us that we have much less control than we desire. The service to individualizing is to ask, "Why might a person assume that way?

- Blaming.

Whereas customizing areas way too much responsibility on ourselves, condemning scenarios way too much concern on others, as an example, we could claim, "I condemn my drinking troubles on my parents; they made me consume alcohol," or "I have reduced self-esteem because my partner left me." The more we stay clear of taking obligation for our self, a lot more we feel helpless and uncontrollable. We might instead believe, "Yes, this was a difficult circumstance. Currently, I take duty for passing it.".

Exercise: Distortions Review

Before you start, review the list of distortions above, and after that, quiz yourself by thinking of a daily example of each kind of distortion and developing a replacement thought for each.

Using Cognitive Therapy: The Daily Thought Record

A tenet of Cognitive Therapy is that we do not improve without practice. A day-to-day thought record is an essential tool that helps us to slow down our thinking to capture and change the distortions that we repeatedly use.

Make a list of your Automated Ideas (ATs) in that situation, and go back to write down the distortions in parentheses. Next, for each Automated Idea, write down a more logical replacement idea.

Defusing

In his brilliant book about Approval and Commitment Therapy (ACT), Get Out of Your Mind and Into Your Life, Steven C.

Hayes, asserts that nearly all persons suffer some kind of extreme inner pain at long times in their lives. The suffering might be depression, stress, and anxiety, drug abuse, or suicidal and self-dislike ideas, and it arises from the battles we wage against our thoughts as we futilely try to get rid of our histories.

Looking at an instance of the instructor (or another individual) that made you feel foolish. It goes on the assault, believing, "What if I am dumb? I've obtained to quit believing that I'm foolish.

Hayes describes this procedure as a blend. We battle so long versus unfavorable ideas, which we assume to be true, that we eventually become known with the concepts. The logical mind functions well in getting rid of outdoor problems. The, even more, we try to remove emotional problems (for example, by believing about the past), the extra integrated we end up being with the past. We can't eliminate the previous occasion. And also, the extra we attempt not to think about it, a lot more we believe concerning it, experience the suffering, and also wind up being the suffering.

You can examine this suggestion. First, think about a white elephant for many minutes. Currently, block out the photo and also try not to consider the white elephant whatsoever. Count how numerous times you believe about the white elephant. Naturally, you will certainly typically consider the white elephant regardless of your efforts to get rid of the suggestion.

Similarly, we might try to escape the pain with avoidance (using compounds, buying, seeing television, functioning, and so forth). This simply works momentarily, and also after that, the pain returns more highly. The, even more, we try to traumatize the discomfort by switching off our feelings, the extra we shed our capabilities for happiness as well as interaction with life. A numerous technique, defusion, can be beneficial.

It implies selecting to completely allow the discomfort in with a kind, welcoming, dispassionate way of thinking. We still get the thoughts, but we genuinely love them from a variety without buying them. It's as if the war remains to the craze, nonetheless, we've marched from the combat zone, and we see the battle from a variety with detachment.

Workouts: Identify the Source of the Pain

1. Keep in mind a pair of unpleasant scenarios from the past that could have damaged your self-confidence somehow. Perhaps you made a wrong choice or lost your calmness. And also having agonizing ideas regarding these scenarios, you possibly experience excruciating feelings, memories, images, or physical experiences when you think of them.

2. Make a note or record of the length of time each circumstance has troubled you.

3. As opposed to trying to remove these issues, obtain them right into your awareness with an open and also soft mindset. You might believe, "These are simply memories."

Exercise: Milk, Milk, Milk.

1. For a few minutes, experience milk in your mind-- exactly how it looks, feels, as well as tastes. You could see it as cool, white, and velvety.

2. Currently state the word "milk" out loud and repeat it a lot of times as you can in forty-five seconds. The meaning falls away from the word, as well as the name just ends up being audio.

3. Take a negative thought regarding on your own that you connect with among the unpleasant circumstances that you kept in mind above. Place the suggestion into a single word, such as "negative," "loser," "stupid," or "immature.".

4. Rate from 1 to 10 just how stressful words is. Price exactly how credible it is.

5. Invite the word and also other elements of the memory into your understanding with total, type approval.

6. Repeat the word out loud as several times as you can for forty-five seconds.

Now, when again, rate just how upsetting the word is. Did the degree of distress linked with this word decrease? Possibly the term has shed a few of its emotional effect, and also words are now just a word.

Exercise: Keep a Journal.

Record the connected ideas as well as resulting sensations (such as "It shows up unfair that she examined me. I felt uneasy as well as uncomfortable. I began to feel that I'm not excellent when I make mistakes").

Workout: Carry It with You.

Make a note of all the "things" going on inside your head. You could attract a photo of a massive head, and afterward, make a note of all the unfavorable thoughts as well as sensations that you bring.

Women Gaining Self Confidence Through Self-Improvement And Positive Thought

It is uncertain why these differences in confidence levels exist between men and women, buy the phenomenon explains why women should work more to construct and keep healthy self-esteem. Women getting self-confidence is a common topic in the self-help world.

Fortunately, however, women can quickly increase their confidence if they are prepared to make some changes in the way they see or think of themselves and life. With the advantages being increased happiness and paving the roadway to more successful relationships with those around them, it is worth the effort.

Easy Tips To Improve Self-Esteem:

-Enhance personal appearance.

The most convenient and quickest method for women to increase self-esteem is to improve their look. While appearances should not matter in a perfect world, this is not an ideal world and a person's appearance is crucial. People respond much better to others that present themselves in a neat, tidy way that says that they care about their appearance.

Luckily, improving one's look does not have to be costly. By investigating low-cost house charm means, a lady can immediately take steps towards feeling better. This increased confidence gives the inspiration to take extra steps towards increased self-esteem.

Doing this correctly needs an understanding of how human beings work. The automatic part of the human brain works to do this by picking out the negative in the environment. The problem is that considering that it is weighted heavily towards the negative if all a woman listens to is her automatic thoughts; she will neglect the positive aspects of her life and become depressed.

All people likewise can select thoughts. If a woman does not know the true blessings of the friends and family that care for her and that all her fundamental needs are met, then she will be predestined to live feeling that nothing in her world is okay, including herself.

-Practice affirmations.

Thoughts determine the way people feel, and, as discussed above, it is essential to take responsibility for controlling these thoughts. Just as it is vital to be appreciative every day, it is also necessary that a lady acknowledges her worth. To increase self-esteem, a female needs to actively and frequently insert positive thoughts into her thought-stream while learning to let go of the negative.

Below is a list of healthy, self-affirming thoughts:

- I am wise.

- I am more than happy.

- I am unwinded.

- I am effective.

- I am capable of.

- I am well-loved.

-Become action-oriented.

Nothing increases self-esteem quicker than achievement. Each day, women should choose a task that they don't want to do - and do it. When all four steps are consistently followed, the outcomes are large magic.

-Cognitive defusion.

Cognitive defusion is a core element of ACT and is defined as the ability to separate one's self-identity from the language of self-concept. Cognitive defusion helps somebody change the relationship she has with her ideas instead of changing the thoughts themselves. This causes the specific to make a shift from taking a look at the world through literal significance to a deliteralized appearance at literal meaning to develop a healthy distance between ideas and reality. Put another way, customers pacify from ideas by viewing their beliefs as "just ideas" instead of considering them to have meaning.

As formerly outlined, exposure to thin-ideal media images causes the development of body image discontentment and unfavorable effect, typically resulting in unfavorable and distorted cognitions about one's body shape or self-regard. Cognitive defusion could act as a useful tool to help people distance themselves from these unfavorable cognitions, creating a healthy range between oneself and one's thoughts. This can be attained by changing the relationship the individual has with their feelings rather than trying to change the emotions themselves.

Cognitive Defusion Intervention

There have been no previous cognitive defusion interventions mainly conducted to avoid the advancement of body image discontentment, body-focused stress, and anxiety and negative affect after exposure to ultra-thin media ideals. Since psychoeducational media literacy interventions have been revealed to be incompetent, and cognitive-behavioral treatments have a more powerful concentrate on targeting pathology in the individual, there is a need to check out new kinds of interventions that might yield more reliable outcomes and be more matched for easier dissemination.

Preliminary studies using ACT to deal with related issues have shown appealing results. Heffner, Sperry, Eifert, and Detweiler (2002) performed a case study using ACT for anorexia, including such methods as the thought parade (to teach cognitive defusion skills) and the funeral meditation (to clarify worths) into the treatment. The treatment was revealed to be effective, with the customer showing a decrease in a lot of anorexic signs consisting of reductions in the drive for thinness at post-treatment.

Masuda, Hayes, Sackett, and Twohig (2004) carried out a study developed to explore cognitive defusion as a tool that might be used to lower the validity and emotional impact of negative self-referential ideas. Everybody was asked to think of an unfavorable self-referential thought and minimize it to one word.

While the people in the defusion condition were provided a traditional cognitive defusion reasoning and then asked to repeat the negative self-referential word over and over for one minute (the "Milk" exercise), all participants were asked to rate the validity and emotional effect of the terms both before and after the intervention. The efficacy and emotional impact of unfavorable ideas in the defusion group were estimated to lower post-intervention compared to the rankings in the diversion group (Masuda et al., 2004).

A comparable research study was carried out in 2009 by Masuda et al., which discovered that repeating of a negative self-referential word for three seconds lowered the pain (however not believability) of the name while repeating the word for 20 seconds decreased both the pain and the validity of the word.

To efficiently execute this cognitive defusion exercise, the term needs to be repeated over and over for at least 20 seconds. A comparable follow-up research study conducted in 2010 by Masuda et al. verified these results and also discovered that the discomfort and believability of negative self-referential thoughts decreased in the cognitive defusion condition but not in the interruption condition.

Deacon, Fawzy, Lickel, and Wolitzky-Taylor (2011) carried out a study comparing a cognitive defusion intervention to a cognitive restructuring intervention, particularly for negative self-referential body image thoughts. The cognitive defusion intervention produced more significant decreases in body image concerns immediately following the reasoning and training compared to the cognitive restructuring intervention (which was more of a standard cognitive-behavioral technique) (Deacon et al., 2011). A cognitive defusion intervention appears to be a perfect match or unfavorable self-referential idea, specifically about somebody's body image frustration.

As revealed in Figure 1, the primary path leading to body image discontentment, body-focused stress, and anxiety and unfavorable effect includes internalizing the thin-ideal due to socio-cultural discussions of thin-ideal media images. In turn, severe direct exposure to these images develops high levels of body image frustration, body-focused anxiety, and negative affect in people who have at first higher levels of thin-ideal internalization.

The intervention will be administered before viewing the thin-ideal images, with the expectation that the individuals receiving the response will be given defusion methods to use when they are exposed to the images.

Research study Hypotheses and aims

The main aim of the present research study was to examine a cognitive defusion intervention in college females who have thin-ideal internalization. It was hypothesized that the group would report that their negative body image thoughts while seeing the thin-ideal media images would be less believable and less distressing than individuals in the control group. It was likewise hypothesized that the speculative group would report lower levels of body image frustration, body-focused anxiety, and negative affect after seeing thin-ideal media images than the control group.

A secondary aim of the research study was to explore standard levels of thin-ideal internalization, weight-related teasing, and self-esteem as prospective mediators in the efficiency of the intervention. Weight-related teasing and self-esteem were included as potential moderators to take a look at these variables in the context of the Developmental Transitions Model of the advancement of body image dissatisfaction (Levine & Smolak, 1992; Smolak & Levine, 1994, 1996; Smolak, Levine, & Gralen,

It was hypothesized that the cognitive defusion intervention would be more useful for people who have higher levels of thin-ideal internalization, have experienced greater levels of weight-related teasing, have lower self-esteem and have understandings of being obese.

Differences Between Body Image Dissatisfaction, Negative Effect, and Negative Thoughts.

A mixed between-within subjects analysis of variance (ANOVA) was performed to figure out the impact of intervention condition on participants' EDI, PANAS (Negative Affect), Negative Thoughts-Distress, and Negative Thoughts- Believability scores across three periods (pre-intervention, post-intervention, and three-day follow-up. A significant time-by-condition result was discovered for scores on the EDI (Wilks' $\lambda =.87$, F [2,47] = 3.66, p = 0.03, $\eta 2=.14$).

This effect demonstrated that people in the cognitive defusion group decreased in body image discontentment gradually. In contrast, participants in the control group remained steady in their level of body image discontentment. The time-by-condition impact for unfavorable effect revealed a trend towards significance, because people in the speculative group also revealed decreases in unfavorable effect gradually, while those in the control group remain stable;

(Wilks' $\lambda=.892$, F (2,47) = 2.85, p = 0.07, $\eta = 0.11$). There were no considerable impacts on unfavorable thoughts-distress score

(Wilks' λ = 0.96, F(2,47) = 1.07, p= 0.35, $\eta 2$= 0.04) or the negative thoughts-believability rating (Wilks' λ = 0.93, F(2,47) =.1.91, p = 0.16, $\eta 2$= 0.08).

Distinctions between body-focused anxiety. Because the PASTAS was just administered at post-intervention and follow-up, independent-samples t-tests were conducted to take a look at differences in the scores of people appointed to the experimental group against ratings of people who were assigned to the control group. A similar pattern emerged at follow-up, with participants in the experimental group reporting substantially lower mean scores of body-focused anxiety (M = 10.92, SD =.7.19) than the control group (M = 18.48, SD = 11.14; t [48] = -2.85, p = 0.006).

To be conversant with previous analyses, a mixed design repeated process ANOVA was also conducted to analyze modifications in the PASTAS at each time interval. No significant interaction results emerged from this analysis (Wilks' λ =.96, F (1, 49) = 2.25, p =.14, $\eta 2$.=.04).

Secondary Analysis.

-Process variables.

A blended design duplicated steps ANOVA was carried out to examine modification in the DDS, the BIAAQ, and the PANAS-Distress at each time point. There were no substantial interaction impacts for the PANAS-Distress score (Wilks' λ =.0.94, $F(2,47)$ = 1.62, p = 0.21, $\eta 2$ = 0.06), the DDS (Wilks' λ = 0.93, $F(2,47)$ = 1.76, p =.2 2.0.18, $\eta\varrho$ = 0.07), or the BIAAQ (Wilks' λ = 0.99, $F(2,47)$ = 0.19, p = 0.83, $\eta\varrho$.= 0.008).

A mixed model blended design ANOVA steps the 12 item version of the BIAAQ was conducted without any substantial interaction impacts (Wilks' λ =.98 $F(2, 48)$ =.39, p=.68,.2 =.02).

Moderating impacts of self-esteem.

Moderation analyses were done to examine the effect of self-esteem on the effectiveness of the intervention.

Various sets of repeated steps designs were carried out using the following predictors: treatment condition (main result) and the interaction term between treatment condition and the mediator (moderated result). An analysis was carried out to analyze the impacts of RSE score on body image frustration (EDI score). =3.11, p = 0.049). Individuals with higher self-esteem at baseline got greater take advantage of the intervention for body image frustration. In contrast, there were no distinctions between conditions for participants with lower self-esteem. Self-esteem did not have a significant moderating effect on unfavorable effect (F [2,92] = 1.52, p = 0.22) or body-focused stress and anxiety (F [1,46] = 1.66, p = 0.20).

CHAPTER FIVE

Self Esteem and Confidence

We find out about the value of self-worth as well as self-confidence each day in the media. They have to do with a total idea (or do not have thereof) in oneself and also one's capability to make wise selections.

What if those partnerships are holding you back? It's typical for us to be in relationships with "the evil one we understand" rather than run the danger of the "unidentified." These can be romantic, friendship, and even household relationships! I've seen this time around without number with people I've dealt with. It damages my heart each time.

By continuously staying in a relationship you know in your heart is not the best for you, you start to destroy yourself, your self-esteem, and confidence. Now, I'm not talking about a quick choice here - one fight, and you're out of there. No! I'm talking about situations where you've attempted to specify your needs, attempted to change your view, but it is not just working!

There's a distinction between running from an unpleasant situation and knowing that a relationship is no longer serving your best interest. By negating that inner "understanding" and choosing to talk yourself into trying to believe "it's OK," you start to no longer hear that voice prompting you. All this leads to is shrinking your confidence and self-esteem.

That voice serves as your guide, call it your instinct, your gut feeling, or perhaps the Holy Spirit! It's meant to be listened to. If you press it down and push it down, eventually it will give up and be peaceful. The challenge with that is that you start to question yourself and question other decisions, not only the ones having to do with this relationship.

It ends up being a ripple impact. Neglecting that guidance in one setting impacts all your decisions. Since deep down, you know you've ignored the great advice that was given to you, you won't trust yourself.

Fear is the perpetrator here. It's simply too scary to think of changing. But I say to you, what if you don't? Do you wish to continue feeling smaller and weaker? Do you want to guess the second every choice that comes your way? Do you want to be unpleasant and lose out on the chance to be pleased if you were to make a change?

You need to see the costs. Let go of that devil you know and concentrate instead on strengthening your self-esteem and confidence by starting to tune back that voice and what is ahead of you.

Confidence and the Traits of Being Confident

Confidence can be found out and supported, and there specific skills that cultivate it. Belief also includes knowing yourself truly well. As gone over previously, confidence is faith in one's self abilities and judgments.

- Confident people acknowledge their imperfections and understand that the course forward is not about keeping other people down but by raising them and accepting them. Can you easily accept people as they are, even those near you? Do you look for the faults in others to make yourself feel much better? Do you need to relate with those who make you look far better?

- Confident people are always good at quickly measuring other people and finding out the complicated situation and social hierarchies. Are you able to assess situations and people quickly to see your most exceptional fit? Do you feel "in touch" with the feelings and needs of those around you? Can you respond actively to the needs of others?

- Confident people are positive. They know how to mitigate doubts, eliminate worries, and how to discover the good even in unfortunate circumstances. They know failure belongs to everyday life, and that clean slates are always possible. Do you feel happy and beneficial more often that unfortunate or upset? Do you have the mental and psychological tools to conquer negative mindset rapidly? Do you routinely feel gratitude for all of the good ideas in your life? As you know, the traits of confidence, you can start practicing some of these traits in your daily life, even when you might not feel good at all.

Through practice, you'll begin to rewire your brain, so that self-confidence actions feel more natural, making it possible for the feelings of self-confidence as you started to act "as if" you possessed these characteristics.

Action Steps

After taking a look at the qualities of positive people, where do you see yourself having confidence? Where are you doing not have in self-esteem? Address the question under each variety, and take note of the traits you need to enhance most. Frequently improving one character will help boost others.

How You Can Gain Self Confidence

Developing a steady self-confidence will give you the power to achieve anything and whatever that you ever wanted. Let's have an appearance at how you can acquire confidence and establish this vital consideration for your success technique.

Self-confidence is the belief in your self that you can do what you wish to be and do what you want to be, the confidence in your abilities and strength of will to achieve your objectives.

1) You need to begin by knowing yourself and accepting yourself for what you are, your strengths, and your weaknesses. By understanding and taking these, you can build on them and acquire self-confidence.

It is just an understanding and experience that separates a weak point from being a strength.

2) By knowing and exercising your strengths, you build on your successes, which in turn increases your self-confidence. By assessing your previous achievements, you establish the confidence to try new things and to improve on what were your limitations and weaknesses. Little successes give you the self-confidence to get more massive achievements.

3) Keep a Success diary and daily file all the successes of the day, both big and small. Bear in mind; it's what is an achievement to you that matters, no matter how little it might appear.

This will work as an inspirational resource that drives you on when you need that extra boost by giving you a record of all the successes that you have attained. Since you've been successful in the past, by seeing these previous successes, you also know how you can get self-confidence.

4) To help you in establishing your weak points and limitations, you need to develop the mindset that there is no such thing as failure, only feedback.

5) Take personal commitment for your development: you are the designer of your self-esteem, and everything comes back to how you treat and drive yourself that will determine your success or failure.

6) Develop a way of little objectives that will cause success and then establish on them. By preparing ahead, you will get self-confidence by understanding that you are ready.

Instead of launch yourself head-on into a new thing that has been restraint, take little actions that give you little triumphs. In time those small successes end up being larger up until after a time of direct exposure and experience of achievements, in what was the previous limitation, you get the self-confidence to go even more and achieve more.

7) Once you have developed a series of successes, raise the bar, get out of your comfort zone, and stretch. Remember, failure is only feedback. You have a history of achievements behind you that have built your self-confidence. Just keep trying, and you will prosper and, when you do, you and your confidence will reach a new level that can be built on.

8) Reward yourself when you get things: Encourage and reward yourself for working and preparing hard. Know that success comes from the preparation and hard work and not supposed inherent skill - it seems to take 10,000 hours of practice for anybody to master something.

9) Avoid negative people and affects; surround yourself with people, and take part in experiences that will verify your self-esteem and build it, establish healthy positive relationships as they will help you to grow and develop.

10) Learn to relax by establishing relaxation abilities and anchor the states of relaxation with your feelings of self-confidence to

something that has shown to you; it could be a word or a method of holding your hands, anything that shows something to you.

11) Learn proper breathing techniques - breathing equally and deeply with the whole lungs. One of the most typical things that happen, when worry starts to take hold, is that we stop breathing. By concentrating on breathing, we can quickly bring ourselves back into a confident mind-set.

By applying these principles, you will quickly see how you can obtain self-confidence to achieve anything and live the life you would like to have.

Shawn Achor, a beneficial psychology professional and preferred author, describes positivity as the Happiness Advantage. He states success is sustained by joy, not the other way. In positive situations, our brains become creatively inclined, positive, favorably prepared, more efficient, and associated with new tasks.

1. Get in a state of strong beneficial emotion.

To become responsive to new ideas, you must first be beneficial. From this location, you can begin repeating your desired qualities in your mind or aloud like a mantra.

Her condition did not show what she was saying, which's how it's going to be when you start doing this type of work. You have to think about it and believe it. There has to be a certainty behind the gorgeous lies you keep telling yourself every day, the ones about what you want your life to be.

2. Focus your mind on the preferred goal.

Ask yourself a question; How would I feel if I had it now? What does that success feel like?

Spend some time to feel what you desire truly. Be positive in your desires. Feel that pride in yourself, that enjoyment of having accomplished your dream.

3. Put yourself.

Make yourself and how you feel the two vital things. You need to have all that you want on your own.

When Sylvester Stallone was broke, he composed Rocky and declined $300,000 for the script, (comparable to $1 million today). If he played Rocky, he said the only approach the studio may use the writing was. "It was ridiculous at the time," Stallone discusses, refusing such an offer.

You are now capable of attaining all that you desire in life, so be positive in your joy and your goals. Self-confidence can be the difference-maker in your success. The essential things other people do not have the confidence to do can be your open the door to a different life.

Your Brain on Confidence

If you transform your brain, enhancing your self-esteem is a cinch. It does have you repeat little habits frequently, so your brain can takes new neural courses. William James first presented the idea in 1890. Still, it was peacefully turned down by researchers who consistently believed the mind is strictly drawn up, with particular parts of the brain managing specific functions.

It shows by practicing repetitive confident practices; you can rewire your brain to produce brand-new neural courses to seal real feelings of confidence. Your mind will change to your routines, and your feelings of self-confidence will follow suit.

Envision this: every time you take affirmative action or picture yourself with confidence being successful, your brain is being rewired.

Common Barriers to Confidence

Previously in this book, you discovered more about confidence--what it is and how it manifests. Now we'll check out a few of the ways we lose our confidence and how low confidence is expressed in our behaviors, feelings, ideas, and appearance. Among the preliminary steps in understanding the source of low confidence is by knowing your confidence barriers, the areas that link you up when it comes to feeling great about your ability to be successful in a particular situation or in basic. To fix an issue, you need to know what it is initially. Everybody's confidence barriers specify to their specific life experiences and outlook; some typical restrictions apply to everyone.

Here are five of them:

Fear -The most common barrier to continual confidence is fear. Perhaps you worry about failure, fear of rejection, or you may even worry about success. Considering that it sets the bar so high and comes with many expectations and responsibilities, you might fear success. The big majority of your worry is fictional. The only place these worries exist is in your mind. Take a minute to consider your concerns that weaken your self-esteem. Are they grounded in any truth? Exists any evidence they will take place? Are you scared of something that hasn't even occurred or isn't going to take place? Even if some part of your fear occurs, it's seldom as devastating or frightening as you are afraid it will be.

Worry and Overthinking- Another barrier to confidence is worry and believed looping. You may always think about looking best, about what others believe about you, or that you may make a mistake or quit working at something. Fret can end up being circular, conventional thinking enhanced through mindless practice. Your brain locks in an idea, and like a gerbil on a wheel, it's challenging to let go. Worry and overthinking develop because you have a state of mind that's far too focused on knowing and partial results rather than on being who you are, living in today's moment, and accepting yourself. When you participated in the action, through work or play, and when you do something to help or serve other people, you do not have time to worry. Your brain is too occupied in more essential things. When you do have downtime and find yourself in the worry cycle again, simply say the word "stop" out loud to interrupt the worry ideas. Switch your thinking to something positive, or engage your mind in reading, writing, assisting someone, or producing. Since it stealthily holds you down and keeps you from living to your capability,

-**Procrastination robs you of your confidence.** Whenever you leave something reversed or wait up until the last time, you will not do what you might have done ordinarily. The outcome will never be as productive or positive. Procrastination makes you feel incapable, but in truth, all you need to do is start. Taking the effort just to begin something is usually the most challenging part. Identify your issues, give yourself a lot of time, and prepare your tasks according to your issues. If you see yourself moving a task to the bottom of the list repeatedly, make a point to put that job at the leading and do it right now. If you continue to put it off, it will continue to drain you of emotional energy. Simply begin, take one little action, and it will bring you to the way of improving your self-esteem that you can do something about it the next time.

Indecision- The ability to make decisions, even when you aren't 100 percent sure, is essential for establishing confidence. Indecision can paralyze you and render you ineffective and insecure. You can change by giving yourself due dates to make a decision and after that sticking with it. Choices rarely consist of a guarantee, so you will constantly feel some danger with any choice. The obstacle is getting comfy with the pain of risk. The majority of the options aren't long-term. You can change your choice if new information recommends changing it. Waiting to decide up until whatever is best will paralyze you. The best time will not come, so choose a friendly budget time and stick with it.

Your self-esteem should accept, even if it's ultimately the wrong one, then to not choose at all.

-Doubt is often the sly offender for all of the other four barriers. Your worry, fret thoughts, and indecisiveness establishes from uncertainty in your capabilities, knowledge, and judgment. If you don't believe in yourself, why should anyone else believe in you? Analyze what you learned from these situations and how you can change them going forward if you have an unpleasant history of making poor decisions or using bad judgment. The majority of the time, this isn't the case. As grownups, we have a great deal of experience to handle our knowledge and discernment. We simply don't trust ourselves. Who understands much better what is best for you than you do? Start to view yourself as somebody with personal understanding and self-knowledge.

You have the responses within yourself, even if you do not rely on those responses. You can turn the doubt around by practicing little acts of self-trust. Choose a manageable situation where you doubt yourself or your capabilities. Then continue with your best judgment despite your doubts. Practice finding a solution for it even when you aren't sure. You'll be exercising your confidence muscle. These typical confidence barriers affect everybody. Everyone experiences fear, concern, procrastination, indecision, and doubt, from time to time. But when these feelings overwhelm our capability to achieve success, enjoy relationships, speak out, or make an income, then they need to be addressed and taken apart. Action Steps Do you see how these confidence barriers have impacted you in the past? You may find patterns of habits and thoughts linked to many of these barriers that undermine your confidence.

Ways For Women to Improve Confidence

Women, generally have a lot to juggle; it is very easy to see why self-esteem and self-confidence can drop - it is not just possible to do everything. Here are little things that every female can do regularly to enhance confidence and get more out of life.

1. **Act as If**: When you fidget about something, feeling insecure, or uncertain what to do in a specific situation, think of a confident person, either someone you know, a well-known

person you like, or just your ideal of a confident female. Imagine what they would carry out in your situation and, after that, only serve as they would. At initially, this might feel weird, but as you get used to pretending to be confident, it will become second nature up until you are no longer acting. You are in fact, confident!

2. **Find a coach or Mentor**: This may be a good friend or relative, a life coach, or just someone you appreciate. Observe their body language, speech patterns, actions, and day-to-day routines.

Get assistance from their positive outlook to improve your confidence.

Ask for help: Women have so much on their plates; work, family, friends. We can not do it all as well as do require assistance. To truly enhance self-confidence, you must feel you are deserving of help.

Ladies are expected to raise the children (a permanent work itself), chef, keep a wonderful home, bring in a wage, look good, as well as a lot more. We can refrain from all of it without assistance. To improve self-confidence, you need to understand you need help.

4. Exercise: This commonly is up to an all-time low of our priority list because of time restraints, yet I can not highlight enough how helpful it is. Exercise launches feel-good hormones, giving us an instant boost; it makes us really feel a lot more positive concerning the means we look and also gives us more energy. You don't require to pump iron in the gym; choose a vigorous walk, hem and haw your room, or buy a missing rope to make use of in your garden. Thirty minutes 3 times a week will make a substantial distinction to your self-confidence as well as energy degrees.

5. Maintain clean: We are not all supermodels (and also that wants to be anyhow ?!), yet all of us have exceptional functions that we can highlight. Make your hair, put on a mild makeup, and also gown well. This makes a large difference to just how you feel about on your own, which will certainly be mirrored in your perspective, feelings, and confidence levels.

6. Challenge internal negative thoughts: We often have an irritating internal dialogue operating of negative ideas can not do it," it is mosting likely to be a disaster', 'no person respects me' ... How lots of do you have? When you hear these unfavorable thoughts, identify them, and also test them. I'm so fat, well, I might be a little obese, however, I'm consuming a healthy diet and also exercising, so becoming slimmer and also fitter each day. I'll never get it all done becomes, well there is a whole lot to do, I'll do the most crucial initial and ask somebody to assist with the remainder of it does not all obtain done!

7. Stand high: Body language has a considerable effect on both just how we feel and how others perceive us. Stand right, stroll with confidence, make eye contact with others, smile, and also talk gradually and clearly.

These are just of the essential tips that will help to enhance confidence instantly as well as completely. However, you require to take an activity. So rise and do some leaping jacks, put your lippy on and also prepare yourself to feel wonderful

CHAPTER SIX

Identify your Stressor

Over the years, it's been discovered that self-esteem is the common denominator of lots of women's concerns. With better self-esteem, ladies are much more able to discover balance, handle Stress, and claim their freedom.

Globally, females are taken into consideration inferior to guys, and also although our society is changing, most ladies experience damaged self-esteem, even reliable ladies. Self-esteem affects our relationships with others and our connection with ourselves.

A mother might applaud her kid and attempt to impart self-confidence, but if hers is low, undoubtedly, it will be revealed in her habits, and children discover most by emulation.

Balance is an ongoing battle for women. As individuals, as caretakers, as professionals and earners, finding a balance between our feminine and masculine sides, between material and the spiritual a between work and family, and between personal needs and those of our companies, children, parents, and partners need self-esteem and autonomy. Instead of acknowledging how much they attain, women generally are self-critical that they are not getting enough at work, as moms, homemakers, children, or in their ventures. They feel somehow guilty when they don't meet their need and other's expectations. The reality exists isn't enough energy and time to walk around, but how we think about it and assign our resources makes all the difference.

Women are used to stress - taking care of kids while cooking, cleaning, and talking on the phone. Working mothers have added pressure, and it's a difficulty for them to create time on their own. According to the newest census, 55 percent of mothers (63 percent of college-educated mothers) with babies work. Out of mothers under the age of 45 without infants, 72 percent remain in the labor force.

Self-esteem encourages women to practice self-care and to stabilize these contending demands, helping to reduce stress and allowing them to be present to loved ones and any job at hand.

Relationship loss is the most significant stress factor for women, as is a failure for men. When women genuinely value themselves, they are more able to declare their autonomy. Many women complain that they do excellently when they're alone, but as soon as they're in a relationship or the presence of their partner, they lose themselves.

Attachment is significant for women. One reason autonomy is hard is that women don't need to separate from their mothers to become women. According to Carol Gilligan, womanhood is defined by attachment, and feminine gender identity is threatened by separation. On the other hand, because young boys must separate from their mothers and cleeve with their fathers to eventually become men, their gender identity is threatened by intimacy.

Autonomy's opposite, codependency, is typical among women. Lack of independence and self-esteem can trigger many symptoms, such as stress, addiction, domestic violence, and psychological abuse, communication issues, concern and anxiety, regret, anger, and depression. In short, women's health suffers.

The Common Causes of Anxiety and Depression In Women Today

Anxiety can happen to anybody. There appear to be more women suffering from depression and anxiety than men. It's really that many reasons activate depression, but among women, hormones, Stress, and vitamin supplements (or mainly, the lack thereof) is determined as the leading causes of anxiety.

Hormonal Imbalance

Hormonal agents do a lot of remarkable things in the body. You can not have more or less of them to be right at the peak of your health. An imbalance in your hormones can cause a variety of changes in your system. Yes, it can trigger anxiety, amongst many other things.

Women at different phases in their lives are particularly susceptible to stress because of hormonal activity, which can become abnormal during teenage years, menstrual periods, pregnancy, post-pregnancy, and menopause.

Stress

Most women are, by nature, a lot more emotional, the reason why they react more to various kinds of stress, financial and otherwise. Women have to deal with stress every day, but unlike men who simply dismiss certain things, women go out of their way to cope or solve with a particular problem as much as possible

Vitamin Supplementation

Despite the significance of vitamin supplementation, women frequently take this for granted as they focus more on things they think about more vital than their well being - kids, family, career. They don't know that vitamins and minerals play a huge role in managing and preventing anxiety. Specialists have found a link between stress and the absence of specific vitamins, most notably the B vitamins, and Omega 3 fatty acids.

Treatment Options for Depression

Treatment should be begun as soon as possible to prevent anxiety from getting severe or uncontrollable. To find the most appropriate treatment, your doctor will primarily determine what led you to the state.

Hormone Injections

If your irregular hormonal agents are causing your anxiety, your medical professional may put you on hormone injections to manage them in the hope of managing your stress. Not every woman out there will be certified to take hormonal injections, however, as they add contraindications and special preventative measures.

Stress Management

Your physician is likely to suggest stress management, possibly with medications, if Stress is the causative aspect of anxiety. It is essential that you keep stress well under control and not let it manage your life. Here are some exciting ideas to control stress:

-Shop till you drop. Well, why not? What lady will decline the idea of shopping? Simply do not max out your charge card, or you'll have more issues on your back. Shopping, browsing, that is, is Stress alleviating. You don't need to buy anything, even if it is on sale. Shopping offers you a specific adventure and keeps you exhilarated, making you forget (if only short-term) your stressors.

-Take up dance lessons. Wear your dancing shoes and dance your worries away.

-Vitamin Supplementation

On the other hand, if the lack of vitamins is what triggered anxiety, then all you need to do is to ensure you are getting adequate B vitamins and Omega 3 fatty changing. If it is possible to refrain from doing it by changing your diet to include food products abundant in these vital components, your next best choice is to take in vitamins and fats that are of the highest quality.

Why Women Suffer From Depression

Though hormonal agents play an essential part in women's health issues, in the particular case of depression, the main reason why it impacts women more than men exceeds that.

Regarding the recognized biological causes, there are premenstrual issues, infertility, and pregnancy, postpartum anxiety, and menopause (particularly throughout the period causing it). There are sociological and psychological factors for this personality over men.

The role that society designates them is among them. Despite all the women's rights movements that guarantees her a more central place in the financial world, upbringing and cultural impacts are too strong in some cases. Hence, women find themselves having a hard time with the roles of mom, spouse, and professional.

Other factors are psychological or physical abuse, relationship dissatisfaction (might it be marital relationship or just a dedicated relationship) and hardship (a more common stress factor among women who are single mothers).

One essential factor is something that maybe might be deemed a great coping mechanism: women's propensity to consider over a topic always in their heads and with their friends, looking for the reasons for things that happen to them or to get sympathy from their lady friend. Although it is good to vent, the recurrence of this practice can cause anxiety in women to become worse easily.

Regardless of unique aspects that make women more vulnerable to depression, one truth is the same: it is a treatable condition, and once identified, it requires immediate action.

It is very crucial to pay attention to the way we feel. If you feel moody, irritable, unfortunate, or tend to sob for no factor, try to write how often it occurs. You may be establishing a depressive condition and just fall for the old stigma yourself and think it is just PMS. You do not need to feel that way even if that was the situation, there are choices out there to make you feel much better.

Nearly every woman in this world deals with anxiety and Stress in everyday lives. Unfortunately, there are times when people find it challenging to deal with demanding situations.

This might lead to numerous different mental and physical problems. While some individuals try to handle stress and anxiety via alcohol and drug addiction, others become addicted to their medications.

To get rid of stress and anxiety signs in women, you do not need chemical compounds or medications.

There are several ways to handle stress and stress and anxiety without medications and addictions. You can use a lot of stress and anxiety, reducing ideas, and take a holistic method to deal with some anxiety signs in women.

Taking a holistic method is the best method for efficient management of anxiety conditions. Before we discuss this method, let us take a look at the different stress and anxiety signs women experience.

Common Anxiety Symptoms in Women

Many people experience episodes of anxiety in which they feel some or all the anxiety signs noted below. The trigger plays a significant function in separating panic or health anxiety from persistent stress and anxiety.

For example, when you think you heard an unusual noise in the middle of the night, it is reasonable to wake up from your sleep and see your muscle seizing and heart pounding.

Nevertheless, it is unsafe and extremely unhealthy when you experience these symptoms while sitting in a coffee bar.

Here is a list of some everyday stress and anxiety symptoms most women experience:

- Irrational dread or fear
- Headache and muscle Stress
- Chest discomfort
- Palpitations or elevated heart rate
- Insomnia
- GI Distress/IBS/Diarrhea
- A feeling of chest pressure of fullness
- Shortness of breath
- Nausea
- Hot flashes

- Tearfulness
- Abrupt modifications in body temperature
- Anxiety

It is worth discussing that more than 20% of women experiencing stress and anxiety also experience anxiety. Stress and anxiety is a severe problem and ought to not be left without treatment. We've discussed some efficient things to deal with stress and anxiety signs in women.

Holistic Approach to Manage Anxiety Symptoms in Women

To handle your anxiety symptoms, it is essential to know different situations and people that trigger the problem.

Ensure you keep some distance from these situations and people.

It is likewise essential to find specific ways to prevent such stress factors in your life. When you don't want to take medication for your stress and anxiety condition, you should take a break from specific jobs, regimens, and situations.

You require to focus on restructuring yourself. This will permit you to handle the issue or problem at hand with a new technique and viewpoint.

While attempting to manage anxiety signs in women, it is crucial to analyze how you respond to particular situations. It is essential to focus on various jobs and focus on one thing at a time.

You can even join a support system to deal with some anxiety signs impacting your life. With an assistance group, you will have the chance to share your worries and problems with like-minded people experiencing the same issues.

You must focus on many different things to keep you sidetracked from stress factors when you want to handle your anxiety symptoms without any medication.

Some exceptional Stress management techniques include meditation, exercising, listening to music, chuckling, watching your preferred movie, taking long strolls through the park or beach, and more. Such natural methods can be the best way to handle your anxiety symptoms.

There are some other effective ways to manage stress and anxiety without medication. These include working out routinely, getting enough sleep, great nutrition to the body, and more.

To effectively handle tight spots, your mind and body need to be healthy. For that reason, you need to eat lean get, veggies, whole grains, and fruits to acquire long-term energy.

-Similarly, you need to exercise frequently to give your body with oxygen and allow your brain to run quicker.

-An exceptional method of how to deal with anxiety is to be positive in life. You should avoid stressing excessively. It is crucial to develop a positive outlook on your life.

If you are suffering from persistent stress and anxiety and can't get rid of typical anxiety symptoms in women, you should seek expert help. It is necessary to consult a psychologist or psychiatrist to deal with your problem.

Anxiety and anxiety attack is not something you need to manage all your life but can starting today.

Your Body and Mind Need Stress Relief

When your muscles are tight as rocks, your heart is racing; you're holding your breath, "ah," you need to exhale. You need stress relief now! Most of the time, there is no monster chasing you.

Breathe, all the way down into your belly.

Breathe a few times, through your nose, out of your mouth.

Make the noise "ah" on the exhale. As you do that, your mind and body will relax. Look around and observe, at this moment you are safe. Then breathe once again.

One is a part of your brain called the hypothalamic-pituitary-adrenal (HPA) system, which launches a cascade of chemicals- such as adrenaline, hormonal steroid agents, and cortisol-that speed up your heart rate that helps your brain make a fast decision to avoid pain, and increases glucose in the bloodstream to give you a burst of energy to react. This is your body's natural response to Stress.

When a threat is lurking, that is good. What is not natural is continually dealing with demanding circumstances and difficulties day by day. This is understood as chronic stress and can be damaging to your health. Forty-three percent of grownups say they suffer adverse health impacts from fear, and three-quarters of all doctor's tests are the outcome of stress-related disorders and grievances. Stress is also connected to several significant illnesses and unhealthy circumstances, such as heart illness, cancer, lung illness, mishaps, cirrhosis of the liver, and suicide.

It's crucial to understand how stress can impact your daily life, along with your long-lasting health. Much more notably, we need to discover how to alleviate Stress.

Continuous mind Stress can obstruct your clear thinking. You might discover making basic choices like what to have for dinner or remembering directions to a restaurant are more challenging than in a non-stressed state. Getting your jobs and obligations completed may develop into procrastination.

Persistent emotional stress causes people to be easily frustrated and quicker to lose their temper. They might weep more frequently and spend significantly more time stressing over things and even feeling depressed.

Stress impacts your gums and teeth too. Odd as it might appear, stress might cause you to clench or grind your teeth, typically unconsciously or during sleep.

Your hair might come down with your Stress. When somebody is under stress, his or her hair might go into the falling-out phase of the hair life process. It can occur as much as three months after the stressful occasion, though hair regularly grows back within a year if the stressful situation is decreased.

Stress can increase pressure on your excellent heart work. Stress hormones speed up your heart rate, restrict capillary, and established a pattern that makes the heart and capillary more most likely to overreact when you encounter future demanding occasions. Stress is often associated with high blood pressure, embolism, and in many cases, even stroke.

Your body's immune system, accountable for battling a disease, is reduced under Stress. The thymus gland, among the key players, gets little, limited, and tight under stress, and so doesn't work also. If it appears you always fall sick when you can least afford it, it may be because your stress is suppressing your immune system, making you more prone to disease.

Stress inhibits right breathing, so people with asthma and persistent lung problems often have to get worse symptoms throughout times of persistent anxiety.

In your belly, stress takes its toll on digestion so that you may have increased the occurrence of queasiness, vomiting, and diarrhea, acid reflux, ulcer, or colitis flare when you are under chronic stress.

Stress can cause skin problems, rashes, eczema, rosacea, and acne worse. It is also known to bring on fever blisters.

Stress-related stress in your back, neck, and shoulder muscles can result in pain and swelling throughout your body.

What can you do about Stress relief?

Know the source. Sometimes finding your stressors is easier said than done. In most cases, it will be relatively apparent: a close relationship, tight cash, needing friends, body pain, a miserable workplace, or health issues, for instance.

In other cases, finding the source of your anxiety and stress might be more robust. When you are tired, it's slowing you down and making you feel down in the dumps, and you need more rest. When there is an absence of positive, healthy communication between you and a good friend or you are experiencing disputes in a relationship, it can talk through what each person needs that will dissolve the Stress. When we have a financial problem that is haunting our costs routines now, and when you are stressed over every bill and expense, that stress, that dispute, that sinking feeling is stress in action. In that case, seeking approval of what is, and discovering a balance between economizing and taking pleasure in small things in life. At the same time, your financial resources improve from previous mistakes will eventually lower the sense of stress around your situation.

One thing to remember is: often underneath not feeling well physically; there is unresolved anxiety, anger, Stress, or aggravation that we have not been dealing with the right way.

It works to ask ourselves carefully, exists something I am anxious about? What right action can I need to create some level of resolution?

Is there something I am scared of in my life today? What action can I take to feel more secure?

Is there something I am upset about in my life? What action can I take on my behalf today or this week?

Is there something I am annoyed about in my life? What action steps can I start today to change that frustrating circumstance now, or gradually?

What can I do to relieve stress in my life?

The answer is, each day, focus a little time and attention on de-stressing your life. Taking small actions that make you smile, or make you feel more relaxed, or help you get rid of burdens and mess, all these contribute to your health and wellness.

Choosing what you take into your mind, life and body makes a difference: picking healthy food, water, people, dedications, activities all these helps your health, peace, and joy.

Set concerns each day and every week for your jobs.

-Delegate what you can.

A lot of us always feel behind, but we can be practical about how fast time flies in a day. We can be happy we got some jobs accomplished. Feeling thankful for what we did instead of criticism for what we abstain from doing, that is enough.

-Appreciating and focusing your attention on little moments of caring for our kids, listening to birds, seeing flowers in bloom, feeling the shade of a tree, and thinking I am grateful for this time, will bring a growing number of those pleasing, unwinding experiences for you.

-Take a minute in your day to close your eyes, breathe deep into your stubborn belly, and think I am capable. When you do that, Notice how you feel.

-Request help.

Talk with your spouse, children, moms and dads, good friends, and colleagues. Let them know you're working to limit the quantity of Stress you handle. I want to request help when you need it. Be open to receiving support. Those around you may have faced similar conditions and know that can be of advantage to you. Do not be scared to share your feelings. Often talking through a dispute or an issue assists you in understanding better how you can prevent it in the future.

-Set limits on your commitments. Even though being associated with activities such as volunteering and interacting socially can be satisfying, these consistent demands, in addition to your other family responsibilities, might be more than what you can handle without feeling stressed.

Mounting stress and pressure may start to weigh down your shoulders like a load of bricks. Before you allow it to get the best of you, take a break.

-Feeling tired? Instead of grabbing caffeine for low energy, attempt walking, going outside, and getting some fresh air. Take some deep breaths, concentrating your attention on your back, and breathe out with the sound "ah."

This maybe your best assets in the fight against frustrating stress. They can also assist you in organizing your schedule or letting you vent disappointments about difficult circumstances.

-Make a List.

Believe you can multi-task?- Reconsider.

When the ideas in our head are overruling, the research study suggests we're not as efficient in doing so many things simultaneously as we wish. Where do you begin? Initially, make a list. This helps you see what's on your plate so you can much better acknowledge what can wait and what needs your attention now. Then focus on the products and finish them one at a time. That is enough. You don't need to be super-mom all the time!

Get regular sleep, and eat plenty of fresh fruits and veggies. Choose more frequently to avoid caffeine, alcohol, drugs, and tobacco in favor of natural stress relievers, like a visit to a mountain, park, pond, garden, creek, or in your backyard.

Moving your body is good for stress relief. Exercise of every kind boosts your feel-good endorphins. Moving neutralizes the damage Stress is doing to your body and gets your mind off what is stressing you. If you can't squeeze in 30 minutes each day, Three brief ten-minute sessions are fantastic too. Go for a walk, ride your bike, jog, dive rope, bounce on the kids' trampoline, play tag with your kids, put on music and dance, let's hear your concepts!

It's easy to get lost in the "what if's" of the future, but if you have a backup plan for upcoming demanding events, you will be faced with fewer surprises. Ancient words of wisdom suggest: avoid the threat that has not yet come, that is believe ahead, but many of us live in the present minute.

Make sure you practice some relaxation techniques, such as deep breathing, meditation, yoga, stretching, visualization, and massage. These are all fantastic ways to exercise the physical and psychological impacts of persistent Stress.

Permit a little time to Focus on what you do and like in your life. When you are worried about what you don't like, your stress level increases and more of that seems to appear in your life. Over time this is one of the best Stress relief strategies for your mind and body.

CHAPTER SEVEN

Goal Setting and Planning

Healthy self-esteem is crucial to women's holistic health. Self-esteem issues are the most prevalent psychological health issue among women. Body image is very vital; it is one of the aspects that impact a lady's self-esteem.

The term self-esteem is used to explain an individual's total sense of individual value or self-regard. It is a character trait that includes a variety of beliefs about self, such as habits, emotions, attitudes (practices and attitudes), ideas, and the appraisal of one's looks. Confidence and fulfillment in oneself impact all phases of one's life. This also enhances your self-esteem and self-regard. Humbleness, modesty, and humility assist you in improving your self-confidence. Self-esteem is a sense of individual worth and ability that is fundamental to an individual's identity. Your self-concept has an excellent effect on how and what you feel about yourself. By loving yourself, you improve your self-esteem!

As a woman, the very best way to live a euphoric and beautiful life is to believe in yourself. Every woman possesses the power and potential to live the life of her dream, but many are not because of the issue of low self-esteem. You can increase your self-esteem and enhance your experience and living through these means noted below:

1. Appreciate Your Physique:

Those females you see in the pages of some papers, magazines, and TV ads are typically not realistic representations of genuine women. When you are continually seeing size four women, and you are a size 10, it can make you start feeling unwanted or less right about yourself. Strolling around your neighborhood, you will see women of various sizes, heights, shapes, and colors; know that being sexy and stunning comes in different types, including your own.

2. Have Positive Thoughts and Beliefs:

Change unfavorable and disempowering ideas with life-uplifting and enhancing thoughts. If you believe you are ugly, this will become genuine to you because your mind paints your world. Even if you have committed some errors in the past, forgive and motivate yourself. When things are not going well, relax, and give yourself pep talks. Positive thought, confession, and doing so, yield positive results. Affirm, "I am gorgeous and special!"

#3 Avoid Unhealthy Comparison:

Unhealthy contrast of yourself to another person will just make you feel bad. No two people are the same; every lady is distinct and unique.

Conquering Low Self Esteem

Our beliefs about ourselves impact our feeling on an everyday basis, change how we view life and can misshape our behavior towards others. Many women identify that low self-esteem limits their capacity, stops them from doing the things they enjoy, and causes problems in substantial areas of their lives.

One way of taking a look at low self-esteem is that it is a form of bias we hold against ourselves.

The majority of us like to believe that we do not hold a bias against other people. Nevertheless, we may not understand that we are holding onto an always vital 'inner picture of ourselves, an image which is so distorted that it is, in fact, a kind of prejudice, perilous harm that we are harboring against ourselves.

Again, most of us can see when inhuman treatment is hazardous or weakening for someone else. Many of us would step in to protect somebody we thought was being treated unfairly ... at least, we would acknowledge unjust treatment.

The signs of low self-confidence in women - low self-esteem can reveal itself in some or all of these situations:

-feeling unconfident in social scenarios

-being passed-over for promo at work

-not sticking at studies or projects

-not trying-out brand-new hobbies, sports or interests

-creating regular issues in close relationships

-accepting an uneasy home-life

-not taking care of health

-spending unwisely on unnecessary items

-enabling violent behavior

Some of the more straightforward signs of low self-esteem - thoughts and sensations related to persistent low self-confidence and self-esteem can include:

Constant self-blame, guilt, fear, shame, uncomplimentary comparisons with others, seeing other individuals' behavior towards us as 'proof' of our failure, unreasonable pessimism, playing the role of 'victim' when it could be possible to take more control, perfectionism, obsessing about what other people think, idolizing certain people and making harsh judgments (mainly of ourselves.).

Some less apparent symptoms or indications of low self-esteem are:

Many women with low self-esteem generally take it out on themselves. Some women have informed us about some of the less apparent signs of low self-esteem: being often (or exaggeratedly) cynical about other individuals.

Consistent skepticism of honest people, unreasonably high expectations, fault-finding, micro-managing, setting 'tests' for how much people care, and inability to forgive can be some of the less apparent signs of low self-esteem.

Women also can try to 'puff themselves up' to make themselves feel more significant because of an underlying worry about their real value as a person, and because of unpredictabilities about how important they are to others. Needing to be 'best' all the time, showing-off with the current designer-labels, and bitching or gossiping about other women can originate from an underlying low sense of intrinsic worth 'in ourselves,' or from an exaggerated concern about our value in the eyes of other people.

The behavior brought on by a low self-image can also differ from person to person.

Some women say that having a poor self-image, or low self-confidence triggers them to take ill-considered threats (such as drinking too much in public places). In contrast, others say they avoid required risks to such an extent that they daren't attempt anything new (such as meeting new people or seeking for a better job) even if they really would like to. This can cause loneliness and frustration.

Some women frequently apologize, while some women blame others too much. Some women overlook their appearance; other women spend all their money and time on beauty-treatments and clothing. Naturally, these practices can all be triggered by various things, but a low self-image can be the cause of widely divergent unhelpful, and self-sabotaging behavior.

Close relationships can be affected by low self-confidence. Lots of women find themselves focusing excessively on their partners, possibly by compulsively picking arguments, checking on their whereabouts, showing many irrational signs of jealousy of a trustworthy partner, being over-solicitous, or by being 'clingy.'.

House-work and practices in the work-place can also show imbalanced behavior originating from deep insecurities. Some women over-focus on making the perfect home or overlook their homes because they feel that an uneasy environment is all they are worthy of. Some women push themselves to work penalizing schedules or allow individuals to maltreat them at work (for instance, by hanging promotion that never materializes.).

Low self-esteem can produce a vicious circle - our unfavorable beliefs about ourselves. Our lives can end up being a 'self-fulfilling prophesy.' behavior we embrace to compensate for our low estimate of ourselves as a way of making the opposite of what we truly want and need; it can push away well-meaning people and can even bring in challenging people who will abuse. Women can find themselves looking at a life that shows back to them just an impoverished, distorted, and unappealing photo of themselves. This further boosts their low self-esteem.

Professional counseling and psychiatric therapy can help women (who genuinely want to) to learn how to conquer their low opinion of themselves and live a more satisfying life. Counseling can assist people in changing unhelpful beliefs about themselves and improve their unconfident self-limiting behavior.

Changing unreasonable critical views, we hold about ourselves into something more well balanced and motivating is something that really can be done. We can establish more motivating and realistic beliefs about our capabilities and about the potential our lives could hold for us. Relationships can have more of a possibility to grow and stay healthy, and careers, social-lives as well as interests have a better opportunity of taking off.

The research study of low self-esteem in women has a great but brief history.

We have looked at how low self-esteem establishes, both from early experiences and from more recent events. We have also looked at how low self-esteem can preserve itself by forming compensatory (often dysfunctional) 'guidelines' for how we must think and behave.

This body of work has assisted professional specialists in informing useful guidelines for helping women get rid of low self-confidence. There are now several methods and techniques which women can use to encourage their 'inner critic' to back off sufficiently for them to develop what some counselors call 'Healthy Self Esteem.'

Some practitioners have worked intensively on this issue with a vast array of women. As a result of this in-depth experience, it is now possible to see some of the patterns that have emerged in women's' lives. Counselors have discovered a lot about how to go about improving women's' inner picture of themselves.

Experienced counselors have likewise learned something of value. Certain restorative techniques do not help women with low self-esteem, and can even make a low self-image worse.

It isn't as simple as just 'believing positively,' although this approach, in some cases, assists. For some people, 'Positive-Thinking' strategies can be counter-productive. Three primary healing techniques emphasize a balanced approach to self-esteem: Cognitive Therapy, Pellin Contribution-Training, and Gestalt treatment.

Knowledgeable counselors can help customers develop 'Healthy Self-Esteem' and learn new life-skills.

In dealing with low self-esteem, counselors can assist women in developing well balanced and motivating beliefs about themselves and their lives. It is essential to support women while they are in the process of forming new attitudes and behavior since this can be a screening time. Specialists can gently encourage their clients to test with new and various methods of doing things. It can be efficient to discover life-skills such as Assertiveness and Non-Violent Communication, which make it possible for women to reveal themselves constructively. Reliable counseling can encourage clients to try new beliefs and abilities, with 'baby-steps' at first, and then in more significant methods substantial areas of their lives. (In many ways 'Healthy Self Esteem' is more of a verb than a noun; our self-confidence gets stronger through finding out how to do things in a different way and through assessing the results.) Experienced counselors can 'tune-in' to the specific factors that will assist each woman find the most reliable (and best) methods of conquering their low estimate of themselves. This can free women to be more able to develop lives that reflect a more exact image of themselves, their skills, and their desires.

Are you enjoying this book? If so, I'd be happy if you could leave a short review on Amazon, it means a lot to me! Thank you.

How each person develops low self-esteem in the first place, how we learn to conquer it by establishing healthy self-esteem, and who helped us along the way can be a remarkable story that varies considerably from one woman to another.

Actions For Boosting Low Self-Esteem

As women, we sell ourselves short. Maybe it's because we don't think we'll make up for what the world expects of us. For example, appeal displayed in publications, signboards, and advertisements have everything from cheekbones, waistlines, skin tone, and the sizes of nose, lips, eyes, breast, and buttocks digitally improved. Who can take that in the real world?

We're expected to be the best mom, the perfect spouse, hot, strong, smart (however not too wise), a confidant, friend, flexible, financial wiz, and the list goes on and on. We need to be whatever that everybody expects of us; otherwise, we lose confidence in ourselves. We consume over our "failures" because we believe that our neighbor, sis, co-worker, and every other lady can do it all. Low self-esteem can rollover from our teen years or approach us when we least expect it. We lose confidence, and a few of us, if the fact is told, never had it to fail.

Some reports recommend that women's self-esteem is associated with how her significant other, family, or friends views her. For these women, their self-image problems are out of their control. Women forget far too quickly that self-esteem is all about self-image and total confidence in self.

The good news is that a negative self-image is entirely reversible, but we have to be ready, able, and ready to reprogram our thinking. To begin the process, here are a few ideas for developing self-esteem:

=**Get a new mindset** - Thinking happy thoughts will put you in a better state of mind. Do not state things to put yourself down, but more notably, don't ever allow yourself to think those toxic thoughts.

Anguish is contagious, and if your buddies are unhappy with themselves, it will rub off, even if you do not know it. Sign up with a club, get a new hairdo, and keep your alternatives open for new experiences.

Feelings of low self-esteem are regularly linked with physical looks, such as weight (specifically in women). If you can confess to your negative habits or behaviors, you can take control of them!

=**Set New Goals for Yourself** - Working towards an expert or individual goal can do wonders for your self-esteem. Weight loss (as noted above), going back to school, refining a craft, starting your own business are all things that will help you to focus favorably on yourself.

=**Empower Yourself** - Get your confidence, start believing in yourself, and stop reading for someone to verify you. You may be amazed to find out how many people will be drawn to your self-confidence, including the opposite sex!

= **Don't hesitate to look for counseling** - If you know you have problems that are hard for you to manage alone, you mustn't handle them alone. Discover an expert to work with you when you're ready. Even looking for professional assistance can be empowering.

=**Be Led by Faith** - Whether it is through spirituality or through those that genuinely love you, encourage yourself to be led by the faith that others have in you. You are capable, and you are loveable, and you deserve to be delighted. You do have a gift and emotional appeal, just trust yourself, and you'll find it.

" I CAN is 100 times more significant than IQ."

Way back in the '60s before Woodstock, you had this chart-topper by the Beach Boys called "Good Vibrations." The song goes thus; "In picking up good vibrations, she is giving me excitations." Good vibrations are always connected closely to self-esteem. They mean a significant positive mindset towards life.

You are bombarded with a million images on the television and the internet all of which are intended at telling you how you ought to look, what you ought to use and what you should do to get ahead, how to get a better partner while discarding the present one or how to have better sex. However, below are significant steps towards building a reservoir of self-esteem;

- **Be Positive**

Being positive is the first essential towards restoring your self-esteem. Even though bad things can occur to individuals who are negative and positive, the gung-ho types tend to make the best of a bad scenario.

There are evident advantages in being optimistic and it is related to a positive state of mind and high morale, good health, active problem-solving capabilities, and flexibility from stress. It leads to low self-esteem, which will manifest like some hydra-headed alien through high levels of stress and anxiety, depression, jealousy, relationship break-ups, and an inability to think positively. Negative thinking implies unfavorable vibrations.

- **Be Content with Yourself**

Emotional security can not be purchased at any rate. It comes from within. You are surrounded by the frequently toxic criticism of other people against the world, other people, including yourself. If you are not prepared to deal with it, you are responsible for ending up living in a state of apprehended madness. Or much better still, you can calmly go back like some Jedi knight and handle these "interruptions" by "discovering to be self-sufficient with the deficiency of things." You learn to be content with yourself to be delighted with the way you are. It does not suggest that you start to appear like a frump or letting yourself go to seed, But more than happy about yourself and your self-confidence increases the number of notches.

- **Be Firm and Believe in Your Dreams**

You have to determine what you want in life and then go for it, regardless of what others do or say to discourage you because it is your life, not theirs. I always say you have one shot life on earth; for that reason, make the finest of it. And most essential, never bow down to the pressures of those around you to give up on your dream of being self-fulfilled.

Just believe in yourself and your dreams, they become real.

Confidence is typically explained as a state of being particular, either that a hypothesis or prediction is appropriate, or that a selected course of action is the finest or most reliable offered the circumstances. Lack of confidence in oneself is what stops individuals from getting concentrated on what they wish to achieve at a point in time. That little voice within telling them they can't do something is their biggest unmotivated.

Boosting your self-esteem and confidence can help you in understanding an empowered you, consequently moving you towards your pursuit of success in life.

What can you do to gain confidence?

You have to be confident in who and also who you are. There is no feeling in moving from right here to right here till you brand it in your heart and spirit that you are fearfully and unbelievably made.

Face Your Fear: Is there a particular thing you are terrified of? Face it. Doing something scary and conquering the worry is a superb way to enhance your confidence. Go on, leap out of that plane (with a parachute undoubtedly), drive that lorry, talk in front of a big group, ask for a promotion, or whatever it is that horrifies you.

2. **Love Yourself:** We are typically informed to like others as we enjoy ourselves. Could this be the problem with the majority of our relationships, we do not love ourselves?

This can take little practice and looks amusing, however, try it, it works. Offer yourself a tremendous large hug when you wake up in the morning. Do the same when it's time for rest.

You've heard this claimed a million times before: "How can you anticipate others to love you if you do not love on your own?" It's real. Exercise the very early morning and also evening hugs for two weeks, potentially three weeks if you're the stubborn kind, and you'll see just how fantastic it works.

3. Avoid excuses: You must resist the urge to always make excuses, in other words, the excuses for why you could have, should have or would have. It might sound something like the following;

"If only…"

The above two words have caused shattered dreams, missed opportunities, damaged relationships, and so on. Do the following sound familiar? If I had much more money, if I could dance, if only I had an education like so, therefore, if only I were thinner, if only I might gain more weight, if only I were like so and so.

Life is too short to remain in situations of 'if only'. If you can change it or improve on it, just do it. If not, accept what is and cherish the moments of your life. Live, live, live! Do not come to the last days of your life with a statement like… "I could have lived a complete and remarkable life If only"

CHAPTER EIGHT

Self-Hypnosis, Meditation, and Affirmation for Women

Many people have lost their self-esteem and self-respect. With the economy making havoc in many people's lives, is it any wonder things are the way they are. There are so numerous people unemployed; many have lost their houses and families.

For many, it is simple to quit; after all, it is difficult losing everybody one treasured and loved. I remember an expression I discovered a long time back, "when the going gets tough, the tough start."

1. Do you know your role?

If you can find your life working, you can turn around any circumstance ailing you at the time. There are various stories of people near the brink of total disaster or damage who have found a genuine purpose and turned it all around to be successful.

2. Do you know what your specific worths are?

If you don't know, then how will you reconcile them to your function? Your function and worths require to be lined up. Make a clear list of your values and compare them to your purpose.

3. Do you know what your needs are?

Have you been too chaotic looking after everybody else that you have neglected yourself? Do you know what you require, or are you just pleasing everyone else? Now is the time to start looking after yourself.

4. What are you enthusiastic about?

Exists anything that you are enthusiastic about. Discover a more significant cause than yourself and be involved. There are great deals of places where you can offer your services or time, and by doing so, you will get a better sense of self-worth.

5. Are you living 100% on the outside instead of living from your heart?

Probably you've heard the cliche, 'go within or go without.' Do you take any time to sit silently and listen to what is going on inside?

6. Do you honor your abilities?

What is that thing which makes you who you are? And if you are unsure then ask those near you, you might be shocked what you hear. By sharing what you comprehend and are proficient at, you will increase your sense of self-worth and self-confidence.

7. Have you provided yourself and served others?

We are all part of humanity, surviving in this world as persons, yet at the same time as a family. Have you ever gone back to the family or the world? By offering yourself, you end up being richer in ways you may never have thought possible. Try it and see your ownself

There are several ways you can improve yourself and those around you. Please find your purpose and shine your light so we may all see.

Standing Up For Yourself - What Are Your Limitations?

Do you have a difficult time standing up for yourself? Do you sometimes look like a doormat by flexing to what others want and ruling out your own needs?

Requesting what you need can, in some cases, be self-centered, however by not asking for what you need, you are enabling others to treat you in ways that are less than what you deserve. When you were in the process of growing up, you were taught or handled in manner ins, which exposed you that asking for what you required was not essential, frequently. You were not enabled to reveal your emotions such as anger or annoyance with something, so you held it in and just went with whatever was chosen by others.

By holding what you want or need from somebody, you are producing a deep bitterness inside that will decay and rot till one day you blow up. By not expressing what you need, you are not permitting the other person with whom you are relating an opportunity to understand who you are and not allowing them to react to who you indeed are.

You may be surprised that as you raise your needs, people around you will be more than prepared to respond in turn. Start by practicing with those people with whom it does not imply too much; that way, it will be a bit much simpler to consider that the effects aren't so high.

They may be at first a little stunned and hurt that you are acting differently or changing expectations on them, but if they value you, they will want to treat you the way you need to be treated. You will see that your relationships will be a lot much healthier, and people will respect you more as you begin to raise your specific standards.

Solutions For Success - Create a Vision For Your Life

The first step toward success is simple. You need to determine where you want to go. That's very important.

Success requires a clear map, a vision of your perfect life, weight, relationship, task, or journey. If you wish to prosper, you need first to discover where you are going. You will never reach your place, your destiny if you never choose where you want to go.

The primary activity, then, is to dream. Ask on your own, "What do I want? Where do I desire to go? How do I desire my life to transform? Why is this necessary for me?" Is it possible - or it is as if you're fantasizing! - what do you desire?

Ask on your own, "How will I feel when this happens?" Utilize your creative thinking to feel the sensation, hear the sounds, and see the outcomes of your success. The even more information you include your vision, the more 'real' it will appear to your subconscious.

Your subconscious can not pick if what you 'see' is real or unbelievable, so dream large. Without an unbiased vision or strategy, success has nothing to function towards.

At this preliminary action in the direction of success, don't accept any type of limitations. The only limits or boundaries in your life are the ones you set on your own. Do not allow your insecurity to shadow your vision.

As you dream, it contains aesthetic aid to your itinerary. Place those images on your refrigerator, your shower room mirror, the wall surface in your workplace anywhere that you will see them commonly.

Will you move anywhere if you have not chosen where to go, when to go, exactly how to go, or who will pick you? As soon as you have made those decisions - set the vision - do not tell every person, "I'm going to ... next summer period"?

Even if you have not scheduled the trips or resort yet, you think in the journey as if it is a truth. You start believing concerning the locations you'll eat, the crucial points you'll see, the noise of the waves on the coastline, or the wind in the pines.

Success in any type of various other location functions in the very same way. Create a vision.

Dreams do not enter your understanding unless Spirit is all prepared to aid you in accomplishing them. Stay concentrated on the vision until it ends up being 'real' in you.

How You Can Effectively Live to Your Fullest Potential

Many people get lost someplace on the road to success. Indeed, chasing your dreams can be a discouraging task. It needs a lot of work, a more positive self, and a decision. To get the life inspiration that will suffice for you to reach your goal can be difficult, especially when we talk about applying yourself to the constraints.

Life motivation plays a terrific role in living to your optimum capability. Often, when you are so near quitting, the best life inspiration booster can give you the "push" that will keep you moving forward.

How can you live to your maximum potential? Here are a few of the best life inspiration boosters that will make it easy for you to exceed the restrictions of your abilities:

1. Defining the BIG "WHY,"?

This is the most essential belief in life inspiration. Not knowing the reason you want your objective, or why you do it will be your life's failure. Believe it, you won't achieve success when you are unable to determine why you're chasing it.

For a start, clear your mind of anything.

Reserve all barriers and doubts.

Ask yourself these following crucial questions: Why do I want this goal? Why is it worth defending? Why should I chase it? Don't forget, you must determine a BIG REASON, not merely any reason. A factor that will keep you moving, no matter what.

When specifying the BIG REASON in your goal, you'll surely make it to the objective no matter what!

2. Realizing and Understanding your Potential.

Comprehending your abilities and how far you can extend their limitations will be a fantastic start to be able to live to your maximum potential.

Simply look at yourself as a mold of clay. You'll find an approach to form everything completely when you know how far you can mold it without breaking it. And comprehending your capability will help you determine where to start exceeding its limits and where to stop.

You do not genuinely wish to exaggerate everything and end up hurting yourself physically, mentally, and psychologically.

3. Criticize Yourself and be positive about It.

They will say: "Why should we mesmerize self-criticism? It can cause self-doubt! They have a valid point if you look at it negatively.

When you learn and discover your defect, together with your possessions, you can keep balance effectively in your life. Nobody is perfect and nobody expects you to be one. Contemplate this thought and go for some time: What are your weak points? What mistakes do you make that can cause failure?

Confess to yourself that you are not exceptional enough. Maybe you can discover an individual location (ideally dealing with a mirror) and tell yourself about your corrupt practices. Accept all of it and learn to accept your weaknesses. After doing that, you can consider an approach to make it much better. How can you improve your powerlessness correct errors and stay away from bad routines?

When you have gotten here at the perfect service, state the magic words. Latest things that you need to etch in your heart and mind ..." I CAN and I WILL !!!" By doing this, you'll see that you'll establish some components in your life that will make the difference.

With the help of these three life motivation boosters, you can develop self self-esteem and decision. You can now face any challenge you'll come across in your way to success. And eventually, you will find satisfaction and pleasure in real progress.

"THERE IS NO SUCH WORD AS CAN'T!!!".

" Oh, by the way. YOU are a CHAMPION!!!".

Ten Powerful Ways to Stand Up for Yourself in Any Situation.

Since we are reluctant to make our desires or views known, every passing day, we make dozens of little choices that either benefit us by asserting our ideas or decrease us.

Often it seems more natural to opt for the circulation to prevent possible disagreement. But the reality is that letting people walk all over you can increase feelings of stress and anxiety, and it might ultimately decrease your sensations of dignity and play to your insecurities.

Finding out to stand up for yourself will assist you in organizing your life, believe in your power, and push you to grab your dreams. The more powerful you feel, the more powerful you will become.

Learn to defend yourself in any scenario with these ten positive yet straightforward actions.

1. Practice being authentic and transparent.

It takes practice, but discovering to be open and real about what you are feeling or thinking is the primary step. The moment you get in the routine of making yourself heard without being incredibly defensive or accommodating, people will be more open to hearing from you.

2. Take effective but little actions.

Start taking little actions to stand up for yourself if you are struggling with being assertive. Even just discovering to walk more with confidence-- head held high, shoulders back-- will help you appear and feel more positive. When handling others,

Channel that confidence. This mindset can be useful in all areas of life. Feeling angry at the person who cut in front of you at a mall? Well, ask to move to the back. See an unfair charge on expenses from amongst your company? Call and contest it.

3. When someone attacks, hear them out.

As you grow more positive in revealing yourself, you're also going to have to learn to face those who want to bypass you. You must are calm but assertive if you seem like someone is trying to bully you. Walk the high street but stand your ground.

4. Figure out what's truly troubling you.

Going with the circulation for the functions of not making waves produces more Stress and anxiety for yourself. Facing the issue head-on will empower you to make it better and reduces the control it has over you.

5. Clarify first, without attacking.

It's appealing to take a self-righteous stand, mainly if you are sure you are in the. Instead, take a breath and calmly describe your point of view to them. Just then, can a genuine conversation begin to take place?

6. Practice makes perfection.

When you begin to get an understanding of what it means to stand up for yourself, it's time to practice asking for what you want as often as possible. When someone says something you honestly disagree with, or you feel pushed into doing something you do not desire to do, say something. Research study shows that it takes 66 days to form a new habit, so stick to the brand-new assertiveness for two months, and you might be surprised by the outcomes.

7. Be intentional.

Here's a scenario that many people have found ourselves in sharing space with a messy coworker or a roomie who is a slob. You might have been silent while making more exacerbated at the scenario. It may be tempting to slip into passive-aggressive behavior, such as angrily cleaning the mess or making snide remarks. Try being purposeful instead. Inform the person how you are feeling without being accusatory. Be uncomplicated with your issues. Follow up with a fundamental idea that can remedy the situation, such as: "If you can take a minute to tidy up your room at night, it would be a huge support.".

8. Safeguard your time.

Time is a valuable and restricted product, and yet we often feel pressured to supply it away when we can state no. There are specific moments when you might not have an option, such as when your employer specifies a job has a significant concern.

9. Admit that nobody can revoke you.

You are in total ownership of your actions and sensations. Your beliefs, ideas, feelings, and ideas come from you, and nobody else can tell you what you feel or revoke your viewpoints. If you look to invalidate other individuals' points of view, you are also messing up any possibility for problem-solving or having an open conversation.

10. Bogus it till you make it.

Finding to protect yourself will not happen overnight. It spends some time to grow comfortable with being assertive. While you are in the understanding phase, it may help to picture that you are a star finding out to play a new role.

When you swing from being exceedingly zealous to being too indecisive, there may be times. Discovering to protect yourself resembles riding a bike: Eventually, you will find the best balance.

Women love to feel great and also are appreciated for that they are. We all wish to feel great concerning ourselves. You can utilize these affirmations to really feel safer about yourself and also really feel superb from within.

What are some favorable affirmations for women?

I enjoy being a woman

I like my body

I celebrate my femaleness

My body is doing the most effective it can now

Use words indulge in or value if love seems like a word that is as well strong for now. You may not feel like you can love your body yet, but beginning to appreciate it is an outstanding start.

Looks affect your self-confidence

A woman's appearance can influence her confidence level. The media bombards us with photos of what is 'best', and then we unintentionally contrast ourselves with that said. If our firm believe what they show us is the only sort of being lovely, and also we look various from that, then we may start to develop certain undesirable views regarding the means we look. Progressively, damaging ideas as well as beliefs concerning ourselves restrict us and also generate fear in our lives. We begin to end up being scared of being that we are within.

Just how can positive affirmations assist?

The basis of making use of positive affirmations is that we create our thoughts and ideas in life. These points of view as well as ideas after that develop our reactions to anything that occurs.

Favorable affirmations assist transform your negative thought patterns as well as habitual responses right into even more positive and also self-caring ones. When a negative thought shows up, the secret is to see. If the concept makes you feel great, ask on your own. Choose a much far better one by transforming it about if it does not.

What if it's not working?

Occasionally, you highly establish as well as assume with thoughts and suggestions that you have hung on to for a lengthy time. While such thoughts may have served you in the past, you can allow them to go as well as select brand-new ones that nurture you.

How to Change Negative Thinking and Create a Positive Life

We might find that as soon as one bad thing occurs, we relate it with all the other harmful elements that have happened in our lives and start to feel depressed. We may contact concerned in the present-day, having a difficult time getting out of our heads as we fret and obsess about the things that could go wrong.

If you find yourself in this frame of mind typically, you are what psychologists call an over-thinker, and this method of thinking can be damaging to your psychological and physical health. Psychologists have discovered that over-thinking can result in torment, anxiety, and fatigue, specifically in women, who are more likely than guys to think about dissatisfactions and stress.

In today's society, with negative news coverage, commercials that evoke worry, and all the things happening in the community, it's easy for damaging thought patterns to take root. They often, without understanding it, push away the people that they are concerned about or seeking assistance and motivation from because they can end up being preoccupied, afraid, unpleasant, harmful, and challenging to be around.

Breathe more:

Breathing will relax you, soothe you, connect you to the present moment, and help you feel grounded. It sounds so simple, but typically, when our mind begins to race to wrong locations, we end up being distressed and hysterical when what we need to do is relax the body and mind. One way to breathe more is to use meditation apps, which are easily offered on smartphones and tablets.

We must be conscious of our thoughts since our ideas have power and bring outcomes we may not want, more than we know.

Positive Affirmations for Women - Key Points for Optimal Results

We use affirmations all the time, but we're not even mindful of it - they appear to work under the radar of our awareness, repetitively running in the background and producing the usual outcomes, dictating what we can and can't experience. Repeating a thought is one way in which we form beliefs, and when they're in place, our mind will run them on autopilot so that we can focus our attention in other areas. Learning to drive a car and truck is a good example of this - when first knowing, our attention goes on high alert as our mind needs to process all the components that go into driving an automobile securely. After some months of practicing, we start to feel comfortable driving, and as we enjoy more success, our confidence is bolstered, and we begin to believe that we are indeed a proficient chauffeur. Quickly the ideas and actions needed to drive are permanent, and our mind is now totally free to think and drive of other things. This is the same way in which affirmations lead to our behavior, actions, and emotions, both positively and negatively.

The task before us then is to be mindful of the background beliefs and affirmations we're running, challenge their credibility for us today and if they no longer serve our well-being, remove and change them with positive thought patterns that will assist us in achieving our objectives. Most of the goals women have in today's society are difficult to accomplish - even though the women's liberation movement is now numerous years along, women still deal with the pressures of discrimination, balancing home and career, and a working environment even skewed to desire our complimentary sex. So, to eventually give ourselves the best possible advantage on our paths to success, we must make an effort to tailor our mental/emotional/spiritual disciplines to suit our needs and not the understandings of society - the difference between practicing generalized positive affirmations from a list you find on the internet and personalized, positive affirmations for women designed on your own for your unique scenario, is that by customizing your statements you are actively taking duty for the outcomes you get and addressing the problems that have created scarcity or pain of some nature - you are recovering your power from what you thought had authority over you.

You can do something about it today to get the results you consciously want in any part of your life by applying the following secret points to produce reliable, quantifiable results in your everyday affirmation practices:

1. **Be consistent and persistent:** According to lots of studies taken of participants of self-improvement programs, when pointing out a lack of success in accomplishing their goals, they likewise admitted to a lack of constant practice. This basic key is essential to success - thinking about how numerous years we spend on developing, refining and polishing our beliefs and presumptions

about what we can't do, is it logical to presume that a reversal of understanding is going to occur after 4 or 5 efforts? Research informs us it takes about 21 - 28 days to develop or bring about a new habit. Thus, give your affirmations and goals a minimum of about 21 days before deciding on the level of its effectiveness.

If initially, your affirmations appear to be awkward, forced, or unrealistic - that's excellent! Please appreciate what's happening and use it as fuel to acquire momentum; you can utilize the feelings and ideas about your discomfort to develop a new, empowering affirmation for yourself!.

2. Do it anyway: At the beginning of the exercise, do not fret about whether you believe strongly in your affirmations or not, the effectiveness is in the repeating. Belief in your declarations will develop as an outcome of the repeating and meaning you give your affirmations, so choose wisely. Any resistance that you experience, including ideas about what nonsense all this new age stuff, is, are excuses to keep you free and safe from change. Resistance serves as an opportunity for you to successfully break out of the conditioned responses of the past – endeavor to be

open and see the opportunity in learning something new about yourself; you may be pleasantly amazed at what you find inside!

3. Get clear and well-motivated. The clearer your visions appear, and the higher your motivation, the better your chances will be for achieving your goals. Get all the elements of your ideal life down on paper and be vibrant in your dreams – have many reasons for why you should achieve your objectives; write down all that it will cost you if you don't pursue your dream and all the delight that will result from their achievement. Put your objectives and reasons in point type on a 3" x 5" recipe card and read it frequently, before bed, upon waking and during the day. Create affirmations that reveal these goals and record the passion of your inspirations, and move towards your set goals with a good plan to realize it.

And take off your mind on "how" it's going to happen; that's out of your jurisdiction so do not waste time stressing, fretting or stewing about "what if" or "how" - your Supreme Power has your back so learn to trust, go with the circulation and delight in the ride!

4. Challenge old beliefs. A lot of the ideas we have that trigger our issues of low self-esteem, absence of self-confidence and vulnerability are the results of our early childhood interactions with our moms and dads - beliefs we established as a five-year-old might have been active at keeping us safe and secure as children. Still, that same belief held by an adult can lead to uncertainty or obligation for our joy, to ask for what we want, or be able to state no to others. Ignored, out-worn beliefs that spend time long after their expiry date are accountable for immense discomfort and remorse; find out to recognize them and weed them out of your mind to include new, empowering ones.

For most women, challenging some of the old cultural/ beliefs is especially exposing and empowering as it impacts change not just within ourselves, but also has a trickle-down but for new generations. As we choose to challenge, release, and replace old limiting beliefs about the roles women were traditionally designated to play, we live and teach the new ideas to those that come after us.

The reward is painful old beliefs is that we find that it is our power of choice that frees us from the constraints of the past, and it is our power of choice now that develops a brand-new future to our liking. And restricting beliefs about traditional womanly roles contain terrific product for developing positive affirmations for women to work within manifesting the results they want. Generally, what we want is pretty much the reverse of the belief we wish to drop, so use the old belief and transform it for the positive result you want.

Once released, we can now give the events of the past a new significance and choose to see any conditions as being for our benefit, consisting of the included dimension of establishing new roles for the 21st-century women.

5. Affirm as if it's already done. The essence of this is that our subconscious mind does not know the principle of time - to the subconscious, whatever is now, there is no "yesterday" or "later". Be bold, be simple enough, and be clear with your wordings; always affirm, using positive words in the present tense (not future tense). For example, "I am now talking with confidence and power in the office meetings." contains the outcome of what you're pursuing as against "I will have to talk with confidence and power in the office meetings." The second example is

uncertain as it leaves the result in the future and waters down the goal of learning how to speak up.

The second benefit to affirming as if the outcome has been accomplished now is because it makes it a lot easier to get in touch with your goals emotionally, and mentally charging your affirmations is the secret ingredient to impressive outcomes. This might appear to be a challenge initially, especially if you see yourself feeling any form of discomfort as outlined in the point above, or if you've shut yourself below experiencing a strong emotion. Still, it will genuinely super-charge your outcomes if you can immerse yourself in the feelings, emotions, and feelings of the results you want to be included in your affirmations. Simple repetition works in itself, but the added component of robust, reliable, and positive emotions will accelerate your result substantially. Do not worry if your feelings don't look real, keep it up, be consistent, and you'll enjoy the sweet benefits of your faith and determination.

Applying the five key points of being constant and consistent to offer ourselves the best possibility at success; of believing your vision by doing it even when you feel uneasy because you know positive change is taking place; of being clear about your goals and giving reasons to keep you on course and move you through the difficult times; of courageously challenging outdated beliefs that hold us back and reclaiming our power and control from them; and verifying as though your objective is a done offer to offer your dreams psychological fuel and vigor will give your affirmations the needed weight and authority to power yourself into a future of your intentional development. No one will eventually do this for you, and taking command of your visions, feelings, and ideas is a powerful gift to yourself - enjoy your new powerful and positive results!

Do Self Esteem Affirmations Work?

The whole idea of affirmations is that by repeating suggestive sentences to yourself, you will encourage your brain and subconscious that they hold. For example, by repeating the sentence "I am a confident person" to yourself several times, you will begin to believe it. I can tell you now I've tried this for several years with great deals of variations, I've attempted to tape-recording it on tape and listening while I sleep and it does nothing!

Why Self Esteem Affirmations Do Not Work

The problem behind is that you are sending your brain an extremely unconvincing message since after you complete your self-esteem affirmations, you return to living the life of somebody without any self-confidence. Your mind is observing this and is not convinced at all. Your brain is stuck in thought and behavior patterns, and it will take more than a few self-esteem affirmations to change it, but there are other effective ways to do this.

What Can You Do Instead That Can Build Self Esteem?

So before you were attempting to convince your subconscious that you had self-confidence when you did not. Here is another thought, why not establish confidence in the grand old made way, through taking action and building self-esteem naturally.

That's right, I know it may seem difficult initially, but the best method of slapping yourself conscious out of its old patterns is not to encourage it; you deserve self-confidence, but to reveal it, you deserve it.

Do something that presses you out of your comfort zone, be a generous person, donate some time to charity, be a better friend/partner/parent, take up a new hobby, the list is limitless. Only by living and completely accepting life will you be entitled to the self-confidence you so desire. It is not something that you can 'trick' your mind into giving you; it is established with time and something that you make.

Affirming Your Worth

The initial means to manage the trouble of well worth is to throw it gone. Accept that human well worth is an abstract concept that, upon assessment, turns out to have an exceptionally vulnerable basis. It's simply another international tag. All the criteria end up being subjective, culturally variable, and also harm to your self-esteem. The idea of determining a global criterion of worth is an appealing illusion, however, you as well as everybody else are much better off without it. True human well worth is impossible to determine.

The second method to deal with the problem of worth is to understand that worth exists, however, that it is equally dispersed and also unalterable. Everybody at birth has one unit of human worth, definitely equivalent to everybody else's system of worth. No issue what occurs in your life, no matter what you do or is done to you, your human worth can not be reduced or enhanced. No one is worth more or less than anybody else.

It's interesting to keep in mind that these two alternatives are functionally the same. They both complimentary you to live without needing to contrast on your own to others and make consistent value judgments concerning your loved one worth.

These initial 2 choices are essentially various. The first is a kind of useful agnosticism: someone might or may not be "worth" greater than one more, but this judgment is an unsafe and hopelessly challenging one to make, and also you reject to make it. The second option is extra in accordance with standard Western spiritual teaching, and also results in a comforting, nondenominational "sensation" that individuals deserve something, that they are unique, that they are

more akin to angels than to pets. For the function of fostering self-esteem, you can pick either alternative as well as do well.

The third choice is various from the initial two choices without negating either of them. In this option, you acknowledge your own inner experience of human well worth.

Remember a time when you felt great regarding on your own when human worth appeared actual and also you had an excellent piece of it. You may be, at this moment, absolutely out of touch with the sensation of individual worth.

The factor is to admit that your worth exists, as confirmed by your very own inner experience, nevertheless brief and also occasional it has been. Your well worth is like the sun, always beaming, even when you remain in the color and also can't feel it. You can not maintain it from beaming; you can only keep yourself in the shade by allowing your pathological doubter to throw up clouds of complication or by creeping under the rock of clinical depression.

John, the financial institution supervisor, was able to contact his inner sense of worth by bearing in mind a next-door neighbor he had when he was twelve. She would certainly typically look at John's school tasks and also illustrations when his mom as well as dad didn't have time or were not honest with appreciation. John kept in mind the pride he felt, and also his sense of self-confidence regarding the future.

The 4th way to manage the problem of worth is to take an excellent appearance on your own through the lens of compassion. Compassion reveals the significance of your humanness.

What do you understand concerning yourself? You are living in a world where you should continuously battle to meet basic demands-- or you will pass away. You should discover food, shelter, emotional assistance, rest, and entertainment. Nearly all of your energy goes right into these significant need areas. You do the ideal you can, given your sources. The readily available methods you have for fulfilling your requirements are restricted by what you understand and also don't understand, your conditioning, your emotional cosmetics, the level of assistance you get from others, your health and wellness, your sensitivity to discomfort as well as pleasure, as well as so on. And all via this battle to make it through, you realize that both your intellectual and also physical abilities will undoubtedly weaken-- and also despite all your efforts, you will certainly pass away.

During your struggle, you make many blunders and are compensated with discomfort. Often you feel afraid-- both of really real dangers as well as the vaguer dreads that come from a life without assurances, where loss and pain can slap you down at any moment. There is numerous type of discomfort, and yet you continue, looking for whatever emotional as well as physical sustenance is offered.

In the midst of all the pain, past, and also to come, you proceed to struggle. If you let this awareness saturate in, if you allow on your own truly feel the battle, you might start to get a glimmer of your genuine well worth. As well as the resource of your worth is the effort.

After understanding comes approval. Nothing one performs in the mission to survive is negative. Each method is just much more or less efficient, not agonizing or agonizing. Regardless of your errors, you are doing good work-- since it is the most effective job you can do. Your blunders and the discomfort that follows show you. It is feasible to accept everything you do without judgment because every min of your life you are involved in the unavoidable struggle.

Because you have already paid for them, you can let and forgive go of your errors as well as failures. It is our problem that we do not constantly recognize the most effective way-- and also knowing the method, we might not have the required resources to follow it. Your worth, then, is that you were born right into this location which you remain to live below in spite of the substantial difficulty of the battle.

CHAPTER NINE

Visualization

Visualization is powerful, tried, and tested method for refining your self-image and making important modifications in your life. It involves unwinding your body, clearing your mind of distractions, and envisioning positive scenes.

Whether or not you count on the performance of visualization doesn't matter. Faith in the technique may aid you to achieve outcomes faster than a "nonbeliever," but confidence isn't important to the procedure. Your mind is structured as though visualization functions regardless of what you think. Uncertainty might keep you from attempting visualization, yet it won't quit the method from working when you do try it.

This phase will certainly educate you standard visualization techniques, provide you exercise in developing vivid psychological impacts, and also guide you in developing your very own unique visualization exercises for improving your self-confidence.

Visualization helps to raise your self-esteem in three ways: by boosting your self- image, by transforming the means you connect to others, and by helping you achieve detailed objectives.

If you presently see on your own as defenseless and also weak, you will certainly exercise picturing yourself as solid and clever. If you tend to think of on your own as undeserving and also not worthy, you will certainly develop scenes in which you are undoubtedly a beneficial, deserving specific making a vital payment to your world.

The second step is to make use of visualization to transform just how you interact with others. You see on your own in pleasing connections with your family, your mate, your buddies, and your fellow workers.

Third, you can make use of visualization to accomplish detailed goals. You visualize on your getting that raising, ultimately making that essential degree, relocating into that particular community, mastering your favored sport, making a genuine distinction in your world-- in brief, being, doing, as well as having what you desire in life.

Why Visualization Works

Individuals experience reality indirectly as if they were seeing a TELEVISION screen in their heads. They do not experience the world as it is-- they can just see what's on their screen. And also what's on their display is figured out to a large degree by the power of creativity. This suggests that your body and mind respond in a similar way to imaginary experiences regarding real experiences. In certain, your subconscious mind appears to make no distinction between "actual" sensory data and the vivid sense impacts you summon throughout a visualization exercise.

If you envision on your own freely blending at an event, you will certainly get a boost of self-confidence virtually equal to really going to the event and also successfully engaging. And also the envisioning is simpler, given that you're completely in control as well as experiencing less stress and anxiety.

The affirmations you will certainly consist of in your visualizations act as mindful, positive correction to the negative comments of your pathological doubter. They create a "commentary" component to your visualization as if you were watching a docudrama with a commentator helping to explain what you see on the display.

Obtaining visualization abilities is just a matter of finding out just how to do knowingly what you already do unconsciously. You already produce, modify, as well as analyze what you see on your screen. If you have reduced self-esteem, you probably create scenes in which you are the underdog, edit out any praises, and also interpret much of what you see as evidence of your insufficiency.

You will be able to replace much of this subconscious negative publicity with visualized scenes in which you are the hero, you get well-deserved compliments, as well as you execute capably. In the process of discovering to create dazzling mental images, you will additionally hone your capacity to view fact precisely as well as observe on your own with even more detachment as well as neutrality.

There's one more method of understanding why visualization functions so well to alter your actions as well as your photo of on your own. Think about visualization as a method for reprogramming the way you make straightforward decisions. Join the team by the water cooler or the people at the coffee equipment?

Visualization reprograms your mind to recognize and pick the somewhat a lot more positive of any type of two selections. Gradually, the sum of countless little positive selections is greater self-confidence as well as a lot much more joy.

This programming of your automatic choice production is nothing new. You do it already, however, if you have low self-confidence, you do it backward. You visualize as well as ultimately select the negative course. You see yourself as not worthy, therefore you pick and also expect to be rejected, to lose, to be disappointed, to be depressed, to be nervous, to be assailed by uncertainty and instability. You take the second piece of the pie despite the fact that you are overweight. You are angry at yourself, so you do not use your safety belt, and you attempt to defeat the yellow light. You incline the unfavorable individuals, the excruciating circumstances.

Visualization can change all this. You can utilize it to provide a mindful, favorable push to what has heretofore been an automated, subconscious, and also unfavorable procedure. You can gravitate towards the positive people and emotionally healthy circumstances in which you can prosper and also grow.

Visualize an institution of fish, rushing left and also ideal, backward and forwards randomly. All apply the very same energy to obtain nowhere specifically. If you can become a purposely programmed fish, you can obtain someplace you intend to go, without exerting any more energy than before.

Visualization Exercises

Tip one in visualization is to obtain relaxed. The most effective imagining takes place while your brain is producing alpha waves, which can just happen when you find yourself in a state of deep relaxation. The relaxed alpha state is one of enhanced understanding and also suggestibility.

Do your visualization workouts twice a day. The finest times are just prior to falling asleep during the night and upon stirring up in the morning. You are specifically relaxed and in asymptomatic state of mind at these times.

Guidelines for Creating Effective Self-Esteem Visualizations

See on your own making tiny, positive actions each day towards your objective. See on your walking up to someone as well as asking for a dancing. See on your own using to pass out hors d'oeuvres at a celebration as a way to mingle and also fulfill others.

Visualize obvious habits. Locate pictures of yourself doing something, rather than just looking a certain method, possessing certain abstract high qualities, or having certain points. Maintain asking on your own, "What does greater self-esteem mean to me in terms of behavior? What would certainly I will be doing if I had it? What would my actions appear like, appear like, seem like?" For instance, if you desire to create a photo of on your feeling good about your capabilities, you need greater than a picture of on your grinning-- that photo can suggest anything. Rather, see and also hear on your offering for a challenging however rewarding task. Hear a person matching you on a job well done, and also hear on your own steadily recognizing the praise without any type of self-depreciation.

Include the favorable repercussions of higher self-confidence. See on your effectiveness at work, enjoying closer, and also much more satisfying relationships, accomplishing objectives.

Include assertive, high self-confidence body language: put up stance, leaning ahead to individuals, smiling, arms and legs uncrossed, near to individuals as opposed to keeping your range, nodding as somebody else talks, as well as touching others when suitable.

See yourself struggling a bit in the beginning, and afterward prospering. This method is more reliable than seeing on your own as successful from the initial shot.

See on your liking you extra, not just other people liking you more. The latter follows from the previous, not vice versa.

See yourself as not only "much better" in the future, however also as being generally fine right now.

Assume of self-esteem as something you have, but are out of touch with. See on your own uncovering your self-confidence like a treasure lost and also discovered once more. See dark clouds eliminating to disclose the sunlight that was constantly there. Listen to attractive songs emerging from fixed as you tune right into your self-love. Feel the heat and also gentleness as you pull on a cashmere coat you misplaced and also have simply located.

It's valuable to incorporate visualization with affirmations. Say a short affirmation during as well as at the end of each visualization scene. The affirmation will certainly imitate a hypnotic tip, enhancing the visual, acoustic, and tactile messages with a spoken message right to your subconscious.

An affirmation is a strong, favorable, feeling-rich statement that something is already so.

"Strong" implies that an affirmation ought to be brief, basic, as well as unqualified.

"Positive" suggests that it must not have any type of negatives for your subconscious to misconstrue. Your subconscious tends to leave the negatives, to make sure that "I do not dwell on the past" is listened to as "I do harp on the past."

"Feeling-rich" implies that an affirmation needs to put things in terms of feelings, not theories or abstractions. Say "I love myself" as opposed to "I acknowledge my natural value."

"Statement" implies that an affirmation needs to be a declarative sentence, not an inquiry, an exclamation, or an order.

"Already so" implies that an affirmation should be in today's stressful because that's all your subconscious recognizes. Your subconscious mind is classic, making no distinction between the past, the here and now, and the future.

Right here are some examples of reliable affirmations:

I enjoy myself.

I am confident.

I succeed.

I do my finest.

I have an interest in life.

I am fine simply the means I am

The best affirmations for you will certainly be the ones you compose to match your personality, circumstances, and also goals. Affirmations that you have composed for workouts in various other phases can be adjusted for use with your visualizations.

Bring them into play in your visualization if you have deeply felt spiritual beliefs or theories concerning the cosmos. Do not hesitate to imagine God or Buddha or some icon of global love. You might see yourself treating yourself with regard and tender caring as a reflection of God's love for all mankind. You could imagine a universal love or power streaming with deep space and image your development in self-confidence as retreating of screens that block that energy from reaching you. Imaginatively utilize your beliefs.

As a whole, it assists to see deep space as a place with adequate emotional, physical, as well as spiritual nutrition for everyone-- a kindhearted world that can help everyone. In such a cosmos, all people can adjustment as well as renovation, all deserving of love, all with premises for hope.

Our perception of externals and our experiences in life can transform the way we feel regarding ourselves. The great information, however, is that we can discover out exactly how to establish self-confidence.

In establishing self-confidence, attempts will certainly target ideas, pictures, actions as well as sensations. Which do you think makes the very best beginning factor?

For instance, moms and dad provide an age-appropriate task to a kid, such as obtaining the trash (behavior). When the youngster is successful, she or he is praised as well as believes, "I can do it; the world is reasonable" (thoughts). The child begins to feel positive, which after that brings about extra positive ideas such as "I can do various other things as well as accomplish success." As a result, such a kid might grab an instrument as well as learn how to play it (habits). This, therefore, brings about a lot more positive thoughts, which cause more sensations of confidence, as well as the cycle, continues in a method that strengthens self-esteem. Got the photo? I will typically show this cycle to adults and ask, "So where do you believe is the most effective place to intervene when trying to construct self-worth-- ideas, practices, or sensations?"

People generally react that it is best to jump at the behaviors and thoughts level. Usually, adults choose to start with ideas and habits.

Mindfulness Meditation

Mindfulness meditation has been discovered in recent years to enhance a large variety of mental and medical conditions, varying from chronic pain to stress, anxiety, depression.

Practitioners of mindfulness typically feel more self- positive and comfy in their skin despite external events. Outcomes have been so impressive that mindfulness meditation is now being taught in academic medical centers, discomfort schools, clinics, and health centers (consisting of law schools) all over the world.

This tradition checks out the working of the mind and thinks about how individuals can be better and suffer less. Mindfulness is a lot more than a meditation practice that can have profound medical and mental benefits; it is a method of life that reveals the gentle and caring wholeness that lies in the heart of who we are, even in times of great discomfort and suffering.

The peaceful Tibetan masters have taught that we are of two minds: the ordinary mind and the wisdom mind (Rinpoche.1993).

The ordinary mind and the wisdom mind

The wisdom mind stands for our genuine or true happy nature, which is comparable to the core self. The wisdom mind, like the core illustrated earlier, is kind, smart, and caring-- it desires the joy of others as much as that of ourselves (which is why it enjoys). It is excellent humored, enthusiastic, peaceful, tranquil, and incorporated. The knowledge mind is characterized by self-esteem and dignity, but also humbleness-- realizing that all people possess the wisdom mind.

The ordinary mind supports the wisdom mind just like a dark cloud, keeping us conscious of our true happy nature and causing much suffering (Rinpoche 1993).

The ordinary mind relates to swirling, racing thoughts, and depressing, negative emotions. When certain statements are made like "I am just by myself with worry (or anger)," we mean that we are caught up in the ordinary mind and separated from our wisdom mind. The mindfulness meditation teaches techniques for getting beneath these disorganized thoughts and distressing feelings to rest well in the peaceful wholeness of the wisdom mind.

Kids are not known to experience self-dislike. As we grow older, however, we mostly learn to endlessly think, compare, judge, criticize, blame, obsess about faults, worry, evaluate, and fight against the way life is. We desire that life, or ourselves, turn out differently, and we often get angry when we don't eventually get what we believe we must have. We often fear losing what we already have, and we mostly feel sad when we lose what we believe we need to be happy. Mindfulness teaches most people how to effectively release the ordinary mind's attachments that keep us sad and how to rest effectively in the wisdom mind. Water is allowed to settle when agitated, it becomes very clear. Also, when we let our minds settle properly, we can see clearly.

The attitudes of the heart are very significant in mindfulness meditation. In fact, in a lot of Asian languages, the word used for "mind" is the same used for "heart." Early in the teaching of this technique, Jon Kabat-Zinn (1990) referred to the attitudes of mindfulness.

Heartfulness Attitudes

The crucial ten attitudes of heartfulness, adapted from a work by Jon Kabat-Zinn (1990), recommend a different technique of relating to ourselves and the outside world.

1. **Patience**: Growth takes a very long time. We do not stomp it when we plant a tomato seed. Instead, we carefully put it in fertile soil and make sure it gets plenty of water and sunshine.

We typically can't foresee just how and when our efforts will bear fruit. Or, as another stating goes, "One should wait until night to see how superb the day has been.".

2. Acceptance: This means to take in, or welcome. To accept, then, is to see plainly and with full awareness the bad and excellent, suffer- ing and joy, as part of life, and to experience life without fighting, insisting that things be different, or instantly attempting to change, repair, or get rid of today distress. Even when we are unsure of what to do, we can dispassionately observe, "This is the way things are right now." When we can adequately see the scenario, then we are free to choose what to do-- whether to act constructively or allow the situation to be as it can't withstand it.

We receive them with satisfaction simply as they are when we accept visitors to our house. When we take ourselves, we experience our- selves with a comparable welcoming attitude. We also understand that we are not ideal and also can not will ourselves to be ideal right away. As observed by the psychologist, Carl Rogers, "The curious mystery is that when I accept myself just as I am, after that I can transform".

Wider than self-acceptance, acceptance indicates that we likewise invite the world as it is. In letting go of hostility to unfavorable feelings, we come to be unafraid to feel those sensations. And also when the choice to act ends up being clear, after that we can additionally run with acceptance and also without impulsivity, resistance, or the like.

When we experience discomfort, the natural inclination is to attempt to avoid the pain or do something to eliminate the source of the pain.

If somebody experiences chronic discomfort, one of the worst things to do is to tense up and battle it. Typically learning just to notice the pain, watching it come and go, helps to decrease the pain. Attempting to avoid the pain by running away, sedating oneself with drugs, shopping, watching TV, or using some other type of avoidance just cause the distress to return with higher intensity.

3. Compassion: Possibly the central and most essential attitude, empathy is sadness over the suffering of others, and a desire to help.

In Tibet, compassion is felt towards others and self. He includes that in Tibet, he does not see reduced self-confidence or clinical depression, since individuals there experience empathy towards all people

The following story of empathy tells of 2 young boys that were walking along a road that led through an area. "They saw an old layer as well as a used set of guys footwear by the roadside, and also, in the array, they saw the owner working in the field. Instead of concealing the footwear, they would put a dollar in everyone and see what the owner does when he sees the cash.

Soon the male returned from the area, placed on his coat, slipped one foot right into footwear, really felt something hard, took it out, and also found a silver buck. After increasing up a true blessing on his benefactors, the individual left, and the boys strolled down the road, delighted for the excellent sensation that their compassion had functioned.

Frank Robinson, an experienced player who was recognized by the National Baseball Hall of Fame and also wound up being an appreciated Major League baseball train, just recently needed to pull his third-string catcher out of a computer game in the center of an inning. As rips streamed down Robinson's face at the post-game press meeting, he specified, "I feel for him ... I just value him hanging tough as long as he did. It was not his mistake. Robinson's response was an excellent screen of empathy.

Mother Teresa stated that each detail person had been created to enjoy and be liked. We admire individuals that show concern and also understand how excellent it feels to experience it, both as the giver and receiver.

In our effort to develop heartfulness, we create the objective to be caring towards all people, including our self-- to experience loving-kindness as we struggle to have the strategy to help as we attempt to get over suffering.

Later on, the child discovers out to review as well as judge. Does stating mean things inspire efficiently? An individual who puts him- or herself down discovers it much more challenging to raise.

As a tennis instructor stated, "Sometimes you just have to stop the negative attitude and judgments that obstruct. Just think, 'Bounce, struck.'" Delight in occurs, without evaluating yourself. It can be somewhat liberating to understand that we don't need to panic to scenarios by releasing final, punishing judgments that lead to extremely unfavorable sensations. We merely note what is happening as well as respond in addition to what we can. Do not review the judging if you do discover that you are evaluating on your own or your efficiency.

Thank the common mind for trying to help you improve, and after that calmly bring your account back to what you are doing in the here and now moment.

5. Non-attachment: The Eastern masters show that attachment is the root of sadness. Thus, if I urge that I need a specific kind of automobile to be satisfied, I could be sad if I do not have it. If I get that automobile, I may be scared that it will certainly be harmed. If it obtains scraped or stolen, or I could be mad. If I am connected to my body, my self-esteem could be lowered as I age or add some weight. We can practice loosening our grasp on what we require to have joy and also self-confidence, trusting that we currently have whatever we need for those 2 things. This is not indicated to indicate that taking and valuing care of one's body is useless-- only that externals (money, acknowledgment,

look, roles, and so forth) are not the resource of self-confidence or joy.

In India and Africa, apes are captured by affixing a treat-filled coconut to a string. The coconut has an opening big sufficient for the ape to put his open hand. As soon as the monkey secures his fist on the banana or sweetmeats inside the coconut, the hand is as well big to remove. Resistant to release the hold, the ape can be conveniently caught. In Tonga, the octopus is special. Fishers dangle a basic lure made from a rock as well as shells called a maka-feke from their canoes. The octopus clamps on the method and also is after that pulled into the watercraft. In both instances, the accessory is the issue. Various forms of meditation instruct us to release-- to loosen our grip on the important things that can avoid us from experiencing happiness-- and loosen up into our wisdom minds, where the capacity for joy already exists. Paradoxically, as we launch externals and also quit having a hard time so tough to be something we are not, we obtain a higher admiration of who we are.

6. Beginner's mind: The expert's account is shut to new knowledge and useful experience. The newbie's mind is open to

these. At the competition of this book, you will be asked to approach the skills and also principles used here with an open mind, i.e., the idea of a child who is experiencing something for the first time, without overlying assumptions. Do not immediately think that the way you see on your own can not alter. Try to stabilize a healthy and balanced suspicion with a playful openness to try something new.

Great humor: Much of psychopathology is the propensity to be excessively major regarding our existing problem, to take life as well seriously. As you try the abilities in this publication, please attempt to maintain a trigger of excellent wit as well as playfulness.

8. Commitment: In a caring partnership, one commits to the growth of that partnership. We form an intent (" Shall we appreciate," as an example) as well as try to locate methods to encourage development. In structure self-confidence, we develop a comparable function. When we do not seem like dedicating likewise means that we will certainly exercise the essential skills also as mountaineer William H. Murray specified, "the minute one devotes oneself after that Providence relocates too".

9. Vastness: The understanding mind is substantial, deep, as well as wide enough to contain any kind of suggestions as well as sensations with equanimity. When we are resting in the knowledge mind, it is as if we are rooted in the tranquil, quiet midsts of the sea. From this perspective, we can dispassionately and also compassionately view undesirable concepts and also sensations as though they were waves rising on the surface and after that being absorbed right into the broad sea. This state of mind assists us to be calmly aware without being attracted to harmful judgments concerning ourselves or the situations we experience.

10. Kindness: Despite being among the essential attitudes, kindness is no longer stressed quite in Western cultures, which progressively appear to choose the acquisition and hoarding of material wealth. The generous heart gives a sense of worth, not a need to prove one's worth, understanding that a person's giving matters. Providing can be very easy-- a smile, our full attention, persistence, allowing people to remain just as they are (the gift of acceptance), courtesy, and assisting hand, encouragement, cash, or food-- using what we can, as far as this does not give excessive difficulty for ourselves. What does this pertain to self-esteem? Generosity creates some intangible advantages. We see the joy in the receivers' deals with that makes us feel linked and pleased to others. Giving helps us to let go of accessories as we understand after we offer things away that we are genuinely entire, currently having within us the seeds of happiness. We may think about generosity as practice opening up the understanding fist and releasing things that are illusory or not required for our pleasure.

In some cases, we prevent people who are struggling, fearing that their suffering may contaminate us and drag us down. With that, we close ourselves off from the joy of giving and enjoying.

Exercise: Applying Heartfulness Attitudes.

In a different note, describe a self-esteem issue trouble that you are having. Describe how you may approach this concern using all or a few of the ten heartfulness attitudes. You might discover it valuable to remember times in your life when you experienced or saw these attitudes. For instance, can you think of a time when you were patient with yourself? When were others patient with you or themselves?

CHAPTER TEN

Acknowledge and Accept Positive Qualities

To every woman out there who feels self-conscious whenever you head out, that feels awkward when attempting to strike up a conversation with a stranger, who reconsider to satisfy new individuals, and also especially for those of you that feel like they can never amount to anything, the feeling of being empowered is simply contrary these points! It's the feeling of confidence that you can do anything you establish your mind also!

Yes, the sensation of having the ability to dominate anything is what women's self-confidence is all regarding! It's regarding believing in yourself that you can prosper in your occupation and individual life. It's concerning believing about your abilities to be effective. To be a lot more concrete the empowerment of females leads to having the ability to speak in front of a large group without shivering from phase fright, in having the ability to begin a discussion with someone you just met, as well as usually, in having the capability to eliminate for what you desire and what you rely on.

Here are a couple of tips I would like to share with you if you want this. They're simple, but when they have come to be a part of you, then you're on your way to come to be empowered female that you prefer to be.

Line up versus the wall and feel your back pushed onto it. Standing directly may show up trivial, yet it symbolizes the means you are, the way you see things, and also the method you come close to life. It suggests you're happy with that you are as well as that you're all set for anything.

If you've just come throughout an opportunity or an inspiration that will change your life is you do not look, you never recognize who you'll meet as well as you never understand. Many points occur while en route, and you need to be conscious of them so that you do not miss out on out on anything.

You still require to exercise some tact as being very blunt as well as crass are points you ought to prevent. Know when to make use of a soft voice and also when to talk louder, like when you're outdoors, and there is a great bargain of background noise. Always be favorable and positive things will certainly come to your means.

The first way to handle any concern that impedes your self-confidence is to accept where you are now as a person: every flaw, every pimple, every restriction, and every negative attitude or feeling.

The kind of person you are is very crucial than what you are perceived to be by others. Some of us tend to not recognize that distinction because of the vast amount of marketing and quirks given or fed us, it usually triggers resistance to issues.

Meaning considering that we are taught to act or be a particular way, whenever something comes up, such as a defect that is not expected to be there by social expectation, we tend to press or issues down or resist them.

This resistance triggers out issues to stay, and given that we haven't yet accepted them, they tend to stay there until we deal and accept them.

Remember this - Whatever you withstand, persists! Meaning whatever you resist as not holding true, it will continue to be at the back of your mind and out of your conscious awareness. Once you accept it as being true (there), you can alter it into something else, ending up being aware will bring them to the surface and.

So let's do a fast acceptance workout:

1. Think of a problem, a humiliation, a belief you don't desire, something you have been neglecting till now that merely makes you seem like a cap!

2. Stand up and say with conviction:" I accept that I have (name the issue), and I'm OKAY with it!"

3. Then say: "And I look forward to changing my life for the better by developing more (name the quality you do desire) to enhance the general quality of my life."

When you accept and are okay with something, you'll discover you're far more steady and may even take a growing sense of hope and ability to achieve what you desire.

Accept your flaws and be okay with them and realize its something you can use!

Do this exercise regularly, and you'll discover yourself beginning to feel more clear-headed and capable. You will observe you now feel great about yourself and build a constant growing self-confidence.

Suppose you did this till you are OK with everything, picture! All of your limitations, doubts, negative beliefs, and frustrations that you didn't desire.

Do the workout every early morning and every night for three times a week and notice the difference. When dealing with them, the secret here is that you want to increase your ability to cope with problems and become capable.

After you have done a week, move on top of some other issues that could be troubling you till you end up being strong enough to deal with anything; then, your self-esteem is guaranteed.

CHAPTER ELEVEN

Responding to Criticism

Picture you're painting your bedroom, feeling good about getting the task done. The room looks like brand-new. Somebody is readily available in and also states, "It looks decent. Uh oh, take an appearance at all the splatters on the flooring.

Your state of mind is screwed up. The space that looked so fresh and also shimmering now looks careless and garish. Your confidence withers under the criticism.

The adverse opinions of various other individuals can be dangerous to self-esteem. They suggest or state that you are not worthy in some approach, and you can feel your very own point of view of yourself plummet. Criticism is such an effective deflator of weak self- esteem as a result of the truth that it excites your inner pathological doubter as well as supplies him with ammunition. The critic inside detects an ally in the critic outside, as well as they, join pressures to gang up on you.

Some are even constructive, as it is when the doubter is influenced by a need to help and also formulates the objection in regards to great suggestions for adjustment. Or perhaps your doubter is being manipulative, slamming what you're performing in an initiative to get you to do something else.

Whatever the critic's intention, all objection shares one high quality: it is undesirable. You do not wish to hear it, and you need means to be sufficient brief and avoid it from deteriorating your self-worth.

Criticism has absolutely nothing to do with genuine self-confidence. The trick to handling objection is not to allow it to make you forget your self-worth.

The majority of this phase will manage the approximate, altered nature of criticism. As quickly as you have and understand exercised the skills of discounting objection, you will certainly take place to reliable methods to respond to critics.

The Myth of Reality

You depend on your detects. The earth feels solid. You have uncovered so typically that points are exactly what they appear to be that you have come to trust your senses.

What you anticipate to see and also what you have seen before start to influence what you thought you saw. You see a high blond guy gets hold of a female's bag as well as delves into a tan two-door car and also roar away down the road. The authorities come and also take your statement, and also you inform them exactly what you saw.

The point is that in the warmth of the moment, you can not trust yours detects. Nobody can. All of us choose, change, and misshape what we see.

A TV Screen in Every Head

Many commonly you filter and also modify as if your ears, as well as eyes, were a TV electronic video camera and you were seeing fact on a display in your head. Often the screen is not in emphasis. Occasionally when you are bearing in mind the past, the screen exposes you old film clips, and also you see no "online" reality in any way.

Your screen is not usually a negative point. Without the capability to adjust images on your mental display, you may never before deal with the flooding of information attacking you from the outdoors world. You could never organize and use previous experience.

1, your screen is a splendid device, with great deals of buttons as well as levers to have fun with.

Below are some important policies regarding displays:

Everyone has one. It's how individuals are wired.

You can just see your screen, not truth straight. Researchers educate rigorously to end up being as completely objective as they can. The professional technique is an exact approach to ensure that what researchers are taking a look at is genuinely there and also is truly what they assume it is. The history of science is swarming with instances of genuine scientists who have been betrayed by their hopes, anxieties, as well as desires right into recommending wrong concepts. They mistook their displays for a fact.

You can not recognize what gets on somebody else's screen. You would have to wind up being that individual or possess telepathic powers.

You can not fully interact with what's on your display. A few of what influences your display is the subconscious product. As well as the messages on your screen reoccur much faster than you can review them.

You can not instantly believe what's on your screen. You might be able to end up being 99 percent sure about what's on your display, obviously, you can't be 100% sure. On the various other hands, you shouldn't be so dubious that you do not believe anything you listen to or see.

Your inner self-talk is a voice-over commentary on what you see on the screen. Your self-talk can contain the terrible remarks of your interior pathological critic or your healthy refutations of the doubter. The discourse assesses as well as can batter what you see. In some cases you understand the commentary, however often you are not.

The even more distorted your screen finishes up being, a lot more particular you will certainly be that what you see there is precise. There is no person so sure as someone ill-informed.

You can manage a few of what you see on your display constantly. Merely shut your eyes or slap your hands.

You can regulate all of what you see on your display some of the time. Meditation can take you to an area where you are extremely conscious of just one point.

You can not handle all of what you see all of the time.

You can improve the top quality of the picture on your screen, nevertheless, you can not get rid of the screen. They just knock what they see on their screens. They are never seeing the real you, just their display image.

Your understanding of reality is just among the inputs to your screen. These assumptions are tinted by your innate abilities as well as qualities. Your perceptions can be influenced by your emotional or physiological state at the time. Your sight of fact can be misshaped or hindered by memories of comparable scenes from your past, by your ideas, or by your requirements.

There are various input ports, as it were, through which photos may reach your screen. Just 5 of them have anything to do with truth-- sight, audio, touch, smell, and also taste.

You see a gray-haired guy with wrinkles on his face leaves an automobile and also walks right into a bank. If you have just had a difficult time uncovering a vehicle parking location as well as you're fretted concerning being late for a visit, you will certainly be most likely and cranky to make an adverse judgment of whatever you see. Your experience of banks and also males' design informs you that he most likely has money.

When offered the chance, you might express your objection of this regrettable man to him because it has little to do with the reality, and the whole exchange would be a waste of your time and his. It would certainly be a result of the collection of monitorings, feelings, memories, and ideas.

Display Inputs

In this area we will certainly examine some of the power inputs, besides untainted truth, will define what your screen is displaying.

ALL-NATURAL CONSTITUTION

Some people adapt rapidly to new points, while others prevent adjustment of technology, selecting the traditional, familiar means. Some people are very early morning people, and also some are night individuals. Some individuals can agree little sleep, and also others can not operate without their 8 hours every evening.

These innate character top qualities can promptly color what individuals see on their displays. Night individuals could see a dim, dismal globe in the morning, and also they are more probable during that time to be critical of besides in the evening when they feel stimulated and all set to boogie. Loners consider social functions as something to be endured, while party people see a quiet evening in your house as a stark prospect.

If a person criticizes you for being as well timid and also retiring, perhaps that individual is innately sociable and just view that the means you provide yourself is fine. Or a critic that strikes up at you over little points may have been birthed with an irritable mood, and also his outbursts may have little or absolutely nothing to do with minority little blunders you could make.

People vary significantly in exactly how they refine outdoor excitement. Some are normally "levelers." This implies that when they hear or see something, they immediately, without thinking of it, damp down the experience. It's as though the illumination as well as quantity handles on their displays are completely refused. Other individuals are "sharpeners" that do just the contrary. Their quantity, as well as illumination controls, are shown up high so that every murmur discovers as a shout, every firecracker as a firecracker. A lot of people are someplace in the middle ground. Because they need progressively intense stimulation to surpass their limit of exhilaration, severe levelers are at risk of becoming psychopaths. Severe sharpeners commonly come to be aberrant after years of being bombarded with stimuli that seem too extreme and frustrating.

As well as so no one can be a completely objective critic. You can only slam what is on your screen, and also that picture is not reliable.

PHYSICAL STATE

What you see on your screen can be affected by fatigue, headache, high temperature, belly, medications, blood-sugar degree, or anyone of a hundred physical events.

At first, he didn't observe that he felt or was acting any type of differently than typical. His physiological state was influencing what he saw on his display without his understanding. At these times, he was conscious of his physical state as well as just how it was influencing his behavior, but he could not do anything concerning it up until the drug took hold once more.

If a person frequently nags you, the issue might be an ulcer or a migraine headache, and also not you at all. Your doubter's unpleasant attitude may be a result of eating a suspicious chili dog, not a result of your failing to grab the living area.

MOOD

You see the world with a red haze when you're really angry. The glasses change to the rose-colored range when you are in love. Depressed screens are tinted blue, and also the soundtrack is consistently dismal. If you are what you eat, after that you listen to as well as see what you feel.

How often have you viewed this on TV? The hero functions himself upright into a rage, ultimately tells off his autocratic boss or his unfaithful sweetheart, and then stomps out of the room.

This occurs in reality too, but regrettably without the painless dissolve to the next scene. Usually, you take the force of rage or rejection that has absolutely nothing to do with you. You are as uninvolved as the workplace young boy or the canine. Your only mistake was to be unfortunate adequate to run into the doubter that was still emotional regarding some earlier experience.

Often critics are in a state of basic arousal. They're feeling stressed or concerned or worried by life generally. You cross them in some minor or also thought of away, and also they blow up. Their state of stimulation is revealed as temper, and also their stress is launched for a while.

As an example, your manager chews you out for squandering cash. You got some necessary office products and furnishings, nothing lavish, and you got excellent costs, as well. If your self-esteem is delicate, you might wrap up that you lack judgment which you will certainly never be a success in your work. You might find out later that your employer had actually just obtained a monetary setback and also was feeling specifically paranoid about maintaining expenditures down. There was nothing incorrect with your judgment-- the blowup was triggered by your boss's free-floating state of stimulation, as well as you ended up being a possible launch opportunity.

REGULAR BEHAVIOR PATTERNS

Everyone has dealing techniques that have worked in the past and also that will most likely work in the future. A kid of terrible parents might find out to prevent notification by not talking up, by concealing needs, as well as by trying to anticipate what others desire without actually asking them.

An additional example would be a lady who grew up in a family where an ironic, ironical style of wit was the standard. Outside her household circle, she

commonly turns individuals off. Her regular action pattern of satirizing as well as parodying those around her is taken as a vital, adverse perspective.

Typically when you feel slammed or slighted by someone, you discover later from the critic's friends that "he's constantly like that." What they mean is that his habitual actions patterns lead him to be critical or adverse with some sort of individuals in some circumstances, despite the unbiased fact at the time.

Everybody drags substantial baggage of old behavior patterns around regularly. Generally, people are getting to right into their bag of methods for a familiar means of reacting, as opposed to basing their response on a fresh, precise analysis of the scenario and also your function in it. They are seeing old tapes on their screen as opposed to focusing on the online activity reported by their detects.

BELIEFS

Values, bias, interpretations, concepts, and specific final thoughts about continuous communication can all affect what people see on their displays. Individuals who value neatness may exaggerate all the sloppiness they see worldwide. Those who are prejudiced versus blacks or Jews or Southerners can not trust what they see on their displays concerning the groups they hate. He will certainly often tend to translate participation as a weakness if a man believes strongly in self-reliance. If a lady has a concept that all distressing discouraging causes weight troubles in later life, after that she will certainly see overweight people taking into account her theory, not in the clear light of unbiased fact. When your arms are cross and you rest on the chair while speaking to an insurance salesperson, he might interpret that gesture as resistance to his sales pitch and also redouble his efforts. His view of you on his display will be identified by this interpretation, right or wrong. You could have leaned back because your muscles are stiff or because you wanted to get a sight of the clock.

Ideas are linked strongly to the previous experience of what life is like, what jobs, what hurts, and what helps. She is reacting to her past experiences of people in comparable financial circumstances that either did or didn't pay back their finances. The actual you aren't on her display at all.

NEEDS

Everyone you fulfill is attempting to obtain requirements fulfilled constantly. This vital impacts what people see on their screens. A starving man has an eager eye for food on the table, however might not notice a barking fire in the fireplace or the publications on the coffee table. A woman that feels cold, entering the space, will certainly go right for the fire as well as not discover the food or the publications. A bored individual waiting in the space would take right away on the publications as a source of diversion. A dehydrated individual would certainly discover absolutely nothing in the space to please that requirement and hold a lower point of view of the surroundings than others.

Psychological requirements work the very same means to bring and distort screens on objection that has categorically nothing to do with the actual situation. One more refined example is an acquaintance who is often extremely catty concerning other individuals' appearance as a result of her very own need to be regularly comforted about her physical attractiveness.

The critic reproaches you into doing something that you would not do if you recognized the real reason behind it. His request and also reaction make no feeling to you-- there simply isn't enough work to do to warrant the inconvenience. The actual circumstance might be that your employer is just attempting to thrill his boss by saying that he had a team in over the weekend or that he needs you there to get an important phone call, as well as he's also lazy to come in as well as wait for it himself.

In some cases, doubters are familiar with the psychological demands or hidden programs that encourage them, and also sometimes they're not. Given that you're the individual on the getting end of the objection, their recognition doesn't matter to you. All that matters to you is identifying that needs to misshape a doubter's understanding of reality, and also as a result no criticism can be taken at face value.

Exercise

Consciously make up a narration commentary on what you hear and also see. Visualize numerous possible motivations for what various other people do besides the objectives you assume are proper. It ought to make you realize that there are lots of even more feasible means to see reality than the one you typically make use of.

The Screen as Monster-Maker

The details below mirrors a straightforward, day-to-day experience. Two men meet at an event. One man asks a beginner what he does for a living, trying to make conversation and keep him company. The beginner is here with his partner. These are his partner's friends, not his. He would rather be at home viewing the ballgame or drinking beer with his buddies. He dislikes this type of event and didn't desire to come in the first place. He believes most of his partner's good friends from work are stuck-up pushovers who do not know how to have an excellent time.

The rule for Handling Criticism

The moment you hear an important statement, ask on your own, "What's on this person's screen?" Quickly assume that there goes to best a tenuous, indirect connection to truth. You stand a higher chance of being right than if you think that all essential comments develop from some shortcoming in on your own.

Keep in mind that individuals can only slam what's on their screens and that their displays are not reputable. It's really unlikely that any kind of objection is based upon an exact assumption of you. It's a lot more likely that the critic is reacting to emotions, memories, as well as habits patterns that have practically absolutely nothing to do with you. Since such criticism is a mistake, assuming poorly about yourself. It's like running scared from a youngster with a sheet over his head who pops out behind a bush and claims, "Boo!" You might be stunned initially and drawback, but then you laugh and believe, "It's all right; it's nothing." So with criticism. You may feel quickly taken aback when somebody criticizes you, but after that, you state as well as a smile to yourself, "Boy, I wonder what's on his screen to make him so critical of me?"

Reacting to Criticism

Does all this seem a little impractical? Do you find on your statement, "Wait a minute, some criticism is based on facts. Often the doubter is best accurate, as well as you need to recognize it. Or often you require to defend on your own. You can't just covertly smile and also keep mum!"

You're right if this is what you're thinking. Often you need to react in some method to criticism. The concept "What's on his screen?" is simply a short, but necessary, a bit of initial aid for your self-esteem. Bear in mind that all objection shares one quality: it is unwanted. You did not welcome people to discard the distorted contents of their screen on you. You may even feel that you owe some critics a response, but you never owe a critic your self-worth.

Inadequate Response Styles

There are three standard methods to fail in replying to objection: being hostile, being passive, or both.

AGGRESSIVE STYLE

The aggressive feedback to criticism is to counterattack. Your partner slams your TV viewing practices, as well as your counter with a cutting comment about her love for social media sites. Your partner makes a snide comment about your weight, as well as your counterattack by stating his blood pressure.

The hostile design of responding to criticism has one benefit: you typically obtain people off your back as soon as possible. This is a short-term benefit. They will come back at you with larger and bigger guns if you have to deal once again and again with the same individuals. Their attacks as well as your counterattacks will certainly intensify into a full-blown war. You will certainly transform possibly useful doubters right into destructive enemies.

Even if your aggressive counterattack prospers in shutting a critic up for excellent, you have not necessarily won. If people have authentic grievances with you, they may go behind your back as well as use indirect means to obtain what they want from you. You will certainly be the last to know what is taking place.

Responding to criticism aggressively consistently is a symptom of reduced self- esteem. You lash out at doubters because you privately share their reduced viewpoint of you as well as violently stand up to any kind of pointer of your imperfections. You assault your critics to bring them down to your very own level, to reveal that you might not be worthy enough, you are much more worthwhile than they are.

Constantly counterattacking your critics is additionally a guarantee that your self-esteem will continue to be reduced. The procedure of escalation, assault, as well as counterattack implies that you will certainly soon be bordered by critics who besiege you with proof of your worthlessness.

PASSIVE STYLE

The passive style of replying to criticism is to agree, to say sorry, and to give up at the first sign of a strike. Your partner complains that you are obtaining a little obese, and you collapse: "Yes, I know. I'm simply ending up being a fat slob. I do not understand how you can stand to look at me." Your other half informs you you're following the car in advance of you as well carefully, and you immediately claim that you're sorry, decrease, as well as a pledge never to do it again.

Silence can also be a passive action to objection. You choose to make no response to a criticism that deserves an action. Your doubter after that continues to bug you up until you give some belated verbal reaction, typically an apology.

There are two feasible advantages to the passive style of reacting to criticism. Some doubters will leave you alone when they find that they excite no fight in you.

In the lengthy-term, you will certainly find that many critics enjoy firing fish in a barrel. Your action allows them to feel premium, and also they don't care whether it's showing off at all. And even though you're saved the problem of believing up a verbal action, you will observe that you spend more on mental power in thinking up purely psychological antiphons.

The real downside of the easy design is that surrendering to others' adverse points of view of you is deadly to your self-worth.

PASSIVE-AGGRESSIVE STYLE

This style of replying to objection combines some of the most awful aspects of both the aggressive as well as the passive styles.

When you are first criticized, you react passively by apologizing or concurring to alter. Later you get back at with your critic by forgetting something, failing to make the promised change, or taking part in a few other secretly aggressive actions.

For example, a male slammed his better half for unclear out an accumulation of books and also magazines. She assured me to box them up for the Goodwill vehicle. After being reminded two times to do it, she did call the Goodwill and contribute. While she was at it, she chose some old garments from the closet, consisting of a favorite old shirt of her partner's. When he got angry regarding her offering his preferred t-shirt away, she apologized once again, stating that she didn't recognize that it was so crucial to him, and also if he was so fussy he can call Goodwill as well as manage it himself next time.

In this example, the lady was subconscious of any kind of plot to obtain also. You make reasonable errors. You prepare a unique supper to make amends with your sweetheart, but you fail to remember that she hates lotion sauces.

Easy aggressiveness lowers your self-worth twice. Your self-confidence obtains taken down one more fix when you discreetly strike back.

A continually passive-aggressive response design is difficult to change because it's indirect. The passive-aggressive person finishes up as well terrified to run the risk of open conflict, as well as the various other person has had all depend on and self-confidence destroyed by duplicated acts of sabotage.

Effective Response Styles

The efficient method to react to criticism is to utilize the assertive style. The assertive design of reacting to criticism does not strike, surrender to, or mess up the critic. It deactivates the doubter. When you respond assertively to a doubter, you improve misconceptions, acknowledge what you take into consideration to be accurate regarding the criticism, overlook the rest, as well as put an end to the unwanted strike without compromising your self-confidence.

There are 3 strategies for responding assertively to objection recommendation, clouding, and penetrating.

Acknowledgment. Recommendation indicates merely concurring with a critic. Its purpose is to quit criticism instantly, as well as works quite possibly.

When you recognize criticism, you claim to the critic, "Yes, I have the same image on my display. We are enjoying the very same network."

When somebody criticizes you and also the criticism is precise, just follow these four simple steps:

Say "You're right."

Reword the criticism to make sure that the doubter makes sure you heard him or her properly.

Give thanks to the critic if proper.

While you are working on increasing your self-worth, the ideal plan is never to say sorry and seldom discuss. Remember that objection is unwanted and unwelcome. Most doubters shouldn't have either an apology or an explanation.

Below's an example of reacting to criticism with an easy acknowledgment:

Criticism: I desire you'd be more mindful of your points. I discovered your hammer existing in the damp grass.

Action: You're right. I must have put that hammer away when I was through using it. Many thanks for finding it.

This is all that requires to be claimed. No description or apology or promise to reform is needed. The participant acknowledges a minor lapse, many thanks to the critic, and also the case is shut. Below is an additional example of a basic recommendation:

Criticism: You almost ran out of gas heading to function this early morning. Why didn't you fill-up the tank the other day? I do not see why I constantly have to be the one that does it.

Reaction: You're right. I observed we were short on gas, as well as I must have obtained some. I'm sorry.

In this instance, the participant has caused the doubter some actual hassle and also adds an honest apology. Here's an additional instance of a case where some explanation remains in order:

Criticism: It's nine-thirty. You are supposed to have gotten here an hr earlier.

Response: You're right; I'm late. The bus I got on this early morning damaged down, and they had to send out one more one to pick all of us up.

Advanced acknowledgment entails transforming a critic into an ally. Here's an example:

Objection: Your workplace is a mess. Exactly how do you ever find anything in right here?

Action: You're right; my workplace is a mess, and I can never locate what I want.

How do you assume I could rearrange my filing system?

CONCLUSION

By taking out time to read this book, you've exposed a deep longing to end up being the person you really would love to be and the person you were created to be. Indeed, you have taken a remarkable step towards having better self-esteem. Very few individuals take control of their lives this way and take personal responsibility for experiencing change.

Low self-esteem shouldn't necessarily be your fate or a life sentence. You are not automatically entitled to excellent self-esteem but you simply need to accept it to experience fulfillment in this world of ours. Now you know to empower you and the required tools to work with. You can now see yourself more plainly-- what's been holding you back and how to move forward.

Days or even weeks after the complete reading of this book, it will be quite easy to slip back into old habits, attitudes, and points of view. Your automatic responses to life's troubles or fearful situations will attempt to sneak back in.

You've invested years taking those negative steps but simply a short time trying to undo them. You'll need to remain dedicated and committed to practicing the new skills you have learned and the new methods of thinking you've adopted. Continue taking steps to achieve your goal of having high self-esteem.

Over time, the self-esteem mindset will be your new fallback position. You will see that lifestreams and drops with great times and frustrations, but your self-esteem remains steady.

I am leaving you with some tips and next actions as you advance your journey towards improved self-esteem. Have it in mind that, seldom are your beliefs or thoughts about yourself the truth, the whole truth, or nothing but the truth. Endeavor to challenge your negative thoughts with evidence to the contrary and substitute old thoughts with new, positive thoughts.

Recognize that you are not alone. Everyone has suffered or still struggles with low self-esteem at one point or the other.

Play to your strengths. Acknowledge them and be grateful for them. Work on your weaknesses, but see them as kids who need your love and understanding, not shaming. In life, everyone has areas of strength and weakness. Individuals simply choose to focus on one or the other. *

Acknowledge the role that past events or negative occurrences have played in your current life experience, however, don't remain stuck at that point. Do all that is required to heal from trauma, but remain concentrated on the reality of the present moment, in addition to the goals you wish to achieve.

If anxiety or fear prevent you from taking action, make getting much better your very first priority. Don't put this off. You can't become a person with high self-esteem if you are constantly feeling depressed.

If you suffer from "approval addiction," do all you can to set yourself free from people-pleasing. When you approve of yourself, others (who matter) will be naturally drawn to you.

Keep your operating system and core values in a place where you can refer to them frequently. If you remain true to these in your choices and actions, you can't go wrong. Make practical use of these every day.

Regular exercise makes you feel much better about yourself just as eating healthy, socializing, spending time in nature, linking with your spirituality, and being imaginative. Practice one of these things, when you are down.

No matter how you feel! Be calm, and stop stressing your head. If you are vulnerable to negative thinking, practice the "rubber band trick" and re-frame your thoughts. Go do something. Action is creative and moves you forward.

If you want to feel great about a skill-- practice, practice, practice. Nothing improves self-esteem like mastery and achievement.

Revisit the techniques in this book every day, till high self-esteem feels natural for you. Keep notes or a journal about your objectives, actions, and accomplishments towards your goal. Remind yourself of what you have achieved and what you wish to deal with. Keep this book as a lifetime tool to help you stay on the self-esteem track.

Remind yourself of the fact that life is short and your days are numbered in this world. It is a finite number, and one day you will reach the last number. How many of those remaining valuable days do you wish to give away to self-doubt, anxiety, and fear? For how long will you hold yourself back? Every day, try as much as you can to psychologically put your fears and doubts in a box and put them up on a rack. Make every day look precisely the way you desire it-- without the presence of doubt and fear. One day you'll revisit this box and find it's empty. Because you were too busy living a confident life, your doubts and worries have disappeared.

Indeed, you have something very important to offer the world, your immediate community, and your loved ones. It's been my pleasure to support you on this path by helping you appreciate the confident and incredible individual you are.

Thank you so much for acquiring this book. I'm honored by the trust you've positioned in me and my work by choosing to improve your self-esteem with the knowledge provided.

If you enjoy this book, please let me know your thoughts by leaving a short review on Amazon. Thank you!